THE CRAFTY ART OF PLAYMAKING

The Crafty Art
of Playmaking

ALAN AYCKBOURN

faber and faber

First published in 2002
by Faber and Faber Limited
3 Queen Square London WC1N 3AU
Published in the United States by Faber and Faber Inc.
an affiliate of Farrar, Straus and Giroux LLC, New York

Typeset by Faber and Faber in Sabon
Printed in England by Clays Ltd, St Ives plc

The extracts from the following plays are reproduced by kind permission of
Casarotto Ramsay Ltd: *Just Between Ourselves*, *Relatively Speaking*,
Season's Greetings, *Taking Steps*.

The right of Alan Ayckbourn to be identified as author of this work has
been asserted in accordance with Section 77 of the Copyright, Designs and
Patents Act 1988

A CIP record for this book is available from the British Library

ISBN 0-571-21509-2

10 9 8 7 6 5 4 3 2 1

To the countless theatre people I have worked alongside, for most of whom much of this will come as nothing new: writers, directors, producers, designers, administrators, stage managers, technicians, casting directors and, of course, the actors who ultimately bring it all alive.

Introduction ix · · · · · · A brief history xi · · · · · · · · · · · **Contents**

I've been asked on a number of occasions if I'd care to write something about playwriting, or rather, more accurately, how I go about playwriting. Slightly less frequently, I've also been asked to write something about directing. I've always declined to do either of these, for two reasons.

First, my approach to both jobs has been extremely pragmatic. I'm rarely one to theorise and when I try, I tend to get myself in the most awful tangle and have doubtless confused many more would-be authors or aspiring directors than I've ever managed to help. I see both activities as purely practical ones that can never in the strict sense be 'taught'. They both rely ultimately on a spontaneity and instinct that defies theory.

Secondly, as my career has progressed over the forty odd years I've been practising it, the two activities, writing and directing, have now merged so completely that these days I find it almost impossible to define where one leaves off and the other starts. In other words writing, for me, is in a sense only the preparatory notes for the directing process; directing is the continuation and completion of the writing.

The following is an attempt to describe, as far as I can, this double process. Some of it is quite probably unique to me and contains procedures and practices that it would be highly unwise for others to try and copy. The rest is really just plain common sense. But if I've learnt anything it is that it never hurts to point out the obvious occasionally, certainly in the theatre – to actors, directors or writers and sometimes even to designers, stage managers and technicians. Often we quite wrongly suspect simplicity. We go digging around in the creative sand trying to make our art more meaningful, somehow 'deeper'. Generally all we do is end up with our heads entirely buried, presenting the audience with our rear ends.

Finally, a mild apology. Most of the examples and illustrations that follow are drawn from my own plays. This, I promise, is not a cunning ploy to induce future students to purchase copies of my plays. It's more an admission that when it came to it, my own plays were the readiest to hand and the easiest to recall. But I'm afraid I've never been much of a one for research. Most basic facts have always eluded me at vital moments and I often find the long trek from the keyboard to my reference shelf far too taxing.

Frequently, I fall back on sheer invention, believing that apart from the one essential truth – namely truth of character – theatrical truth need never necessarily bear any relation to real-life truth whatsoever; on the contrary, literal facts often get in the way of a really good story. After all, such things seldom bothered Shakespeare. A lot of it is about whether it *seems* credible. Theatre's a lot about the *seemingly*. You need to believe it at the time.

So by all means believe some of this book, but never all of it.

I wrote my first play in 1959 whilst working as a stage manager, electrician, lighting designer and sound engineer and aspiring to be an actor. I had joined Stephen Joseph, who was running a series of summer seasons of plays in a highly unlikely venue on the first floor of the public library in Scarborough, in the North Riding of Yorkshire. Probably in order to deflect what he quite rightly diagnosed as an abortive ambition to be a performer, he encouraged me first to write and, a little while later, to direct.

At first these two activities were quite unconnected. Some weeks I wrote and/or acted, some weeks I directed. My own plays were directed by others: the first by Stephen himself and the next two by Clifford Williams.

My directing I confined initially to other people's texts, starting with Patrick Hamilton's classic melodrama *Gaslight*. But by the 1960s, with a revival of my fourth play, *Standing Room Only* (and coinciding with my exit as an actor from the cast lists) I began to direct productions of my own texts; though it wasn't until 1975 (in co-direction with Peter Hall) that I first directed in London, with *Bedroom Farce* at the National Theatre, followed in 1977 by the West End production of *Ten Times Table*.

Along with serving as the artistic director of the Stephen Joseph Theatre, Scarborough, I've been juggling the two careers ever since, though a year or so back I made a decision to slow down slightly and to concentrate my energies rather more on writing and directing my own new plays. The older I get and the longer my career as a writer stretches, the more I come to appreciate the fact that there are still new plays coming.

So where does this process all start? How does a play find its way from an often slight notion to a full-blown stage production involving scores of people pursuing dozens of different disciplines? For make no mistake, the snowball effect involved in the creation of a stage play is a drama in itself.

I remember years ago climbing up to the fly gallery of the Globe (now the Gielgud) Theatre in Shaftesbury Avenue. It was the final night of *Ten Times Table*. The set was due to be struck and a new set brought in and fitted up. This new set was also for a play of mine, *Joking Apart*. For about three days (and some nights) I watched as dozens of stage-hands, painters, electricians, stage managers and prop makers swarmed across the stage, first dismantling one set and then assembling the other. The director in me watched with fascination whilst somewhere inside, the writer was silently screaming: My God, what have I started?

WRITING

This really isn't a choice I consciously make. I certainly don't decide when I sit down to write: today I'm going to write a comedy. Simply, I'm going to write a play. The degree of lightness or darkness is often initially dictated by the theme, but never to the extent that I would ever want the one totally to exclude the other.

There's an old acting maxim, 'When playing a miser, stress his generosity.' The same is true of writing a play, or indeed of directing one. The darker the subject, the more light you must try to shed on the matter. And vice versa.

A few years back, when I was again directing at the Royal National Theatre, we did a hugely successful revival of Arthur Miller's tragedy, *A View from the Bridge*. I think I've rarely laughed as much in a rehearsal room as I did during the early rehearsals, as we searched both for the light, the genuinely legitimate moments of laughter – we found lots – and for speed. Our version apparently ran about thirty minutes shorter than a recent New York production had done.

Conversely, when we came a few months later to my own 'comedy', *A Small Family Business,* the search was on for the darkness that lurked behind the cheery family exterior. (It's actually a comedy about greed, blackmail, adultery, prostitution, organised crime, sexual deviation, murder and teenage death through drug addiction – though we never billed it as that!)

No play worth its salt says nothing at all. It would actually be very difficult to achieve this (though I've read some in my time that do come very close). We often dismiss our light comedies and farces as trivia with nothing to say. With the successful ones, this is generally untrue.

I have a theory that to be genuinely respectable as a so-called comic writer, on a par with an equivalent 'serious'

3

writer, you need to have been dead preferably for a century. By which time, of course, most of the comedy is incomprehensible and can only be laughed at by scholars. Never mind, rejoice in the fact that should you be fortunate enough to write comedy, you'll do very nicely during your own lifetime if you're lucky, and to hell with posterity. Though ironically, if you write a comedy truthfully and honestly, it is possible that the play might still survive because of its truth of observation, long after most of the surface jokes are dead.

But the prejudice exists. I was once asked by a journalist if I ever had ambitions to write a serious play. I think my face must have said more than I intended for she instantly dived back into her notebook and asked me whether I preferred cats to dogs.

From time to time I shall be introducing a few 'rules'. Blindingly obvious most of them but nonetheless worth restating even if there's only one in this entire book that hadn't occurred to you before.

☞ *Obvious Rule No. 1*
Never look down on comedy or regard it as the poor cousin of drama.

Comedy is an essential part of any play. Without light how can we possibly create shadow? It's like a painter rejecting yellow. Yet we're an odd nation. Secretly I suspect we don't really believe we're seeing anything worthwhile unless we've had a really miserable time. One of my West End reviews once read, 'I laughed shamelessly.' Shamelessly? What the hell does that mean? 'Sorry, readers, I went and had a very good laugh in the theatre last night which you indirectly paid for'?

I think if I've contributed anything to the sum of modern playwriting it has been to encourage comedy and drama to exist together as they used to in days of old. Somehow

4

they became separated. We began to describe our writers as 'comic dramatists' or 'serious dramatists'.

There was a time back in the late 1950s when I was in weekly rep, where the pattern was roughly to play a comedy then a drama on alternate weeks. One week it was *Oh, Vicar* and the next *Dark Revenge* (imaginary titles, don't look for them). The comedy would be lit as brightly as possible and performed loudly and broadly and very, very fast. 'Go! Go! Go! Gun for the curtain!' was an expression frequently favoured by one director I worked for.

Next week the drama would dictate that the stage lights be lowered to near pitch-black. The actors would speak softly and slowly and there would be much motionless pausing whilst the audience vainly scanned the darkness for any hint that there was anyone left on stage. It occurred to me then, as a mere humble assistant stage manager, that wouldn't it be nice if someone wrote a slow comedy where the actors spoke normally and the lights were low? And in which someone sometimes cried – or even died.

These elements used to coexist. I don't think anyone referred to Shakespeare very often as 'the well-known comic playwright', even though he wrote quite a number of them.

I remember on one of my rare directorial incursions into classic tragedy, in this case *'Tis Pity She's a Whore* for the RNT, being amazed at the number of genuine comic moments littered throughout this darkest of texts. Moments, I suspect, that some modern directors find inappropriate and either cut or ignore.

But a useful tip, I've found, is that the darker the drama the more you need to search for the comedy. If you don't let the audience off the hook occasionally to laugh when *you* want them to, you'll find them roaring with laughter during moments you didn't intend. One of the endearing features of the human race is that we can't generally keep serious for long. Be thankful for it. If we could we'd probably have become extinct long ago.

The initial idea   This concerns what many refer to as inspiration. The idea, the spark, the moment of ignition. Without which nothing catches fire.

Surprisingly, considering this is an element that can never be taught, the question I am continually asked is, where do you get your ideas from? As if somewhere there is a pile of Extremely Good Ideas which I keep locked away in a cupboard ready for immediate use.

The fact is that like every other fiction writer that's ever been born, I am continually haunted by the fear of the well drying up. Ideas are never produced to order, they cannot be summoned on demand. They simply arrive and present themselves. Or they don't.

The knack is to recognise them when they do occur, for very often, they don't come ready formed – behold, here I am, a full-length play complete with first-act curtain. On the contrary, they come as scruffy disjointed fragments, their potential barely visible. Nonetheless, you would do well to welcome them, for they are too precious to ignore, even the most unpromising of them. Examine an idea, any idea or theme with respect and diligence. Maybe in the end it is not for you but for someone else to write. But be careful what you discard. Store it away. It may be that later this unpromising duckling will re-present itself as a thing of swan-like beauty.

☞   *Obvious Rule No. 2*
Never start a play without an idea.

This sounds very obvious but you'll be amazed at the number of would-be writers I've come across who try. They assume, I think, that if they start the journey, maybe an idea will occur on the way. Perhaps a map of where they're going will blow in through the car window. In my experience this never happens. You set off and after several miles finish back where you started at your own front door on page one.

There is no point in launching into a scene between two characters, however sparkling their dialogue might be, if you have no idea at all what might happen next. Interesting as an exercise, possibly, but useless in terms of ever hoping to construct a full-length play.

Before I arrived as the Cameron Mackintosh Professor of Contemporary Theatre at Oxford, I had invited playwrights of any age or experience to submit work, either still in progress or recently completed. From the forty or fifty entries I received, I selected about a dozen writers whom I felt showed some sort of promise. I had an idea in my head that during the year I would coax them and their work to fruition and, using the funds available to me, direct two or three of the best of them using professional actors. In the end, apart from one, no one seemed to write anything further of any significance during the entire year. The exception was a student who wrote, apparently in the space of a few days, a fifty-minute play of considerable promise which I did produce at the Old Fire Station Theatre. Well, perhaps a one-in-ten success rate wasn't so bad, I reassured myself. But the day after my sole triumph opened its young author broke it to me that he wasn't at all interested in writing anything further and saw his future in television as a researcher. Ah, well.

Obvious Rule No. 3
If you don't have the initial inspiration, put down the pen, put the pencil back in the jar, switch off the computer and go and dig the garden instead.

Amongst the group was a young American student who had written three quarters of a very promising first scene of what she intended eventually to be a full-length play. Indeed it was on the strength of these pages that I had invited her to join us. Every two or three weeks I would meet members of the group in a series of one-to-one tutorials where they would report on progress and discuss the general direction their current work was taking. Early on I discovered, to my alarm, that this particular student had no idea where her play – the characters, the story, the theme, anything – was heading. At first I tried to suggest possible directions. Over the year I came up with dozens. I invited her to come up with ideas. Should she introduce a third, fourth, even a fifth character? Should the two she already had on stage strip off and make love then and there? Maybe that would spark something. Should she have them shoot each other? Anything!

In the end, inevitably, there was no resolution. Despite my pleadings, she refused to start again on a new project, convinced that somewhere there lay a solution to her self-inflicted creative deadlock. I suspect that even now, nearly ten years later, her two characters are still in their imaginary New York apartment, trembling on the brink of the most meaningful adventure of their frozen lives. The Greatest Story Never Told.

On the other hand, as I say, don't reject an idea because it seems at first glance too slight. All ideas are precious, and who are we to be picky? Often a tiny idea can merely be waiting for other embryonic ideas to join it and then suddenly, lo and behold, there they are standing on each other's shoulders, making one big idea.

A common mistake in beginners, on the other hand, is to be so obsessed with content that they are in danger of creating something that is too heavy to move anywhere. In other words you can have too many ideas in one play. The result can be a play in which, although it nobly tackles all the ills of the world – the evils of global capitalism, the brutality of some police states, global warming, third-world exploitation, the dangers of racism, sexism, homophobia – a lot is discussed and nothing much actually happens: it takes several hours to go nowhere and depress everyone.

Anyway, it is my belief that although theatre can touch on themes such as these, call our attention to such issues – even, at best, cause us to empathise, to experience for a second or two what so-and-so must be like – the experience is generally emotional, rarely truly objective. Theatre is filled with people, for God's sake, and whether they're hidden behind masks or buried up to the neck in sand, they refuse to be inanimate. We the audience, with our personal prejudices and irrational preferences, are by our very nature biased, invariably more concerned with how they're saying it than with what it is they're actually saying. We search for identifying characteristics, for clues which relate us to the performers. Even puppets we imbue with a sort of humanity. For unvarnished, untarnished facts, please read the book.

At its most successful, theatre views things from a human standpoint. It is after all the most human in scale of all the performance media. My feeling is that that's also a good place for a dramatist to start, at the human level. As a playwright it may be your intention to build a vehicle to take us to the stars. But do make sure you have people aboard.

Initial inspiration – that essential starting point – comes in all shapes and sizes. Years ago I had the tiniest idea for a situation wherein a young man would ask an older man whether he could marry his daughter. The twist was that the older man didn't have a daughter.

Not much to go on, really, but something. Later, I developed the idea slightly. What if the daughter who wasn't a daughter was in fact the older man's mistress? Now we were beginning to have the makings of a rather promising situation.

Continuing on, what if the older man has a wife who knows nothing of this and what if the younger man were to meet the wife first and start talking about her non-existent daughter? And what if the daughter, appalled that the younger man was there at all, had to embrace the lie that the older man was her father, for fear that if she didn't she would lose the younger man? And the wife had no idea what was going on.

A plot was gradually falling together. A quite promising situation comedy of confused identity.

On the other hand, some years later, a rather heavier theme presented itself. It addressed the question I'd often asked myself over the years: what makes certain people in our society conclude that they are fit to govern? Why are some born with the conviction that they are natural leaders, whilst for others the idea never enters their head? And furthermore, although there are a few leaders who are called and deserve to lead, many – politicians, town councillors, captains of industry, theatre directors – are completely unsuited to leadership. Where did they get the idea that they were fit to lead in the first place?

Conversely, it's probably true to say that some of the people most suited to leading us are precisely the ones who have settled for the quiet life and refuse to stand up and be counted. Which explains to some extent why ruthless dictators and bigots and megalomaniacs often seize the reins: because the majority of us – those silent, non-voting, passive observers – take no steps to oppose them. Once you allow a political vacuum to occur through apathy, you invite extremism. Seeking a quiet, selfish life, many are content to follow anyone who purports to know what they're doing and where we should all be going. Witness the last few decades of British politics.

Theatre for me has always been, in a way, a reflection of life writ somewhat smaller. I have seen actors, trusting souls, follow confident-seeming directors who claimed to hold the secret of life itself, over cliffs of incompetence where the performers' self-confidence and sometimes even their professional reputations were all but wrecked. It was just that the director 'looked as if he knew'.

One actor told me of a group of experienced performers, rehearsing with a new young *enfant terrible*, who arrived in the rehearsal room one morning to find that the stage management had brought in a large shallow wooden box filled with sharp gravel. The actors were instructed by the maestro to remove their shoes and to stand silently as a group, barefoot in the box, for as long as they could endure the pain. They stood obediently for some minutes with just the occasional muffled groan. All that could be heard was the sound of the director's (fully clad) footsteps as he paced the room.

Eventually, the leading actress whispered to her co-star, 'This is agony. This man is an idiot. Why the hell are we doing this?' To which, after a pause, her fellow actor replied, 'Yes, but what if he's *right*?'

Yet how to translate this nature-of-leadership idea into theatrical terms? Two people dressed in black, seated at lecterns either side of the stage, discussing the problem? I think not. A brief history of the twentieth century in thirty-five scenes with a cast of forty doubling as Vietnam protesters and Russian Cold War leaders? Unless you have a hotline to the National Theatre and are pre-commissioned and guaranteed production, this is not a wise path to go down, either. As for subsequent productions in the commercial or these days even in the subsidised theatre, dream on.

Better to consider the problem of how to reduce this sweeping, generalised idea to a smaller, more human scale. One that would incidentally also make the play far more theatrical, immediate and engrossing than the presentation of a series of world events covering hundreds of years by a cast of doubling dozens could ever hope to be. Besides, movies tend to do that sort of thing better.

As you see, I had here the makings of two very different plays: one based on a rather big theme about the nature of leadership; the other a purely domestic, essentially lightweight idea concerning a mistaken father–daughter relationship. Both still very much at the embryonic stage.

Where next?

Construction Preparatory work is vital to all playmaking. A dramatist needs to make certain key decisions. Sometimes the solutions automatically present themselves, on other occasions they need careful consideration.

The questions need to be asked: how, when, where and with whom are you going to choose to tell your story? In other words: *narrative, time, location, characters.* These decisions are made in no particular order and often overlap. Some, as I say, have already been dictated by the nature of the initial idea.

To a certain extent, it is often the narrative which predetermines the where and when. If your story intends to cover, say, the rise and fall of a family dynasty, it follows that events will be spread over several time periods. Also, unless you are extremely skilful you will be looking at a number of different locations. Both these decisions, once taken, will have far-reaching effects, as I will later show. They should be taken with great care.

Let's look at that first idea of mine, the father–daughter one, which was later to grow into *Relatively Speaking*. In this, a situation comedy of confused identity, the decisions were reasonably simple. Since the younger man, Greg, needed to meet both the older man, Philip, and his wife, Sheila, it made sense to set the piece in the older couple's house. All that was needed then was a contrivance to get the girl, Ginny, there as well. Perhaps she was there finally to break off her relationship with Philip? Feasible. There were all sorts of problems presented by that but it would do as an initial working plan.

Some problems at least were looking like solving themselves: namely character deployment and cast size. The play seemed to be presenting itself rather conveniently as a four-hander.

Obvious Rule No. 4   ☞
Use the minimum number of characters that you need.

In modern theatre there is a direct inverse relationship between the size of the cast and the likelihood and frequency of production. This has virtually nothing to do with the relative quality of the plays themselves and much to do with cost.

But it isn't only cost. In virtually every theatre department, economy often equals better art. The fewer the locations, the shorter the time frame, the fewer the characters, the less dialogue, the less scenery, the less everything, the better.

Returning to the narrative problems, it was important that Greg arrived in the house convinced that it belonged to Ginny's parents. How does that come about? Obviously she must have told him it does. Why should she do that? Because she's coming down to break off her relationship with Philip and doesn't want Greg to know where she's going. It's a spur-of-the-moment lie by her, to put the boyfriend off the scent.

Where does she tell him? We are going to need a pre-scene, a prologue before we can start the narrative rolling. With luck, this prologue could be used to serve more than one purpose. More anon.

But how does he get there, to the house? Answer: he follows her. But if he follows her, it means he must necessarily arrive second. And for the sake of the initial confusion of identity it's important that he arrives first. In which case, it's important that although she leaves first, so that he is convinced he's following her, in fact she is delayed so he arrives first. (The plotting is getting rather complicated.)

But that means that Greg finds his way to the supposed parents' house without following her. Which means he already knows the address. How does he know the address? Because he finds it somewhere, written down in her flat, that's why. Which conveniently – wait for it – explains why Ginny tells him it's her parents' address. Which is not a very clever lie because why on earth should someone write down their parents' address? Which makes him suspicious, which is why he follows her. It's getting clearer.

Of course, when he arrives and there's this sweet middle-aged woman, Sheila, he realises Ginny wasn't lying after all and that this *is* her parents' house.

A side effect of all this is that the location question has been solved. A two-set play: Ginny's flat initially, then Philip and Sheila's house. Ah, well. One would have been nicer but . . .

Making a virtue out of a necessity though, since the plot demands two sets, this prologue in the flat does give us a chance to establish the relationship between Greg and Ginny. Once the intricacies of the convoluted mistaken-identity plot start uncoiling, as soon as first he and then she arrive at the parents, there's going to be very little time or opportunity to establish much of a relationship. Events will be moving too fast.

☞ *Obvious Rule No. 5*
They need to care about your characters. (So you should too.)

An audience that doesn't care stops listening in the end. Indeed, they might even leave the theatre. It's difficult to get everyone to care, and some characters defy caring about, but the ones you want them to root for need to have qualities an audience cares about. They can have flaws, certainly – they'd better – but they'll need a certain innocence, a trust, an openness that makes us really want things to go right for them in the end. Whether it does or not is another matter.

Stephen Joseph (never a man to waste words) once defined a comedy as being a play in which someone wants something and eventually gets it, and a tragedy as a play where they don't.

In this particular play, they would probably get what they wanted, but they'd have quite a journey before they got there.

So a two-scene first-act structure seemed to be presenting itself:

Establish boy–girl relationship.

Boy finds address.

Boy – establish suspicious nature – suspects the girl is up to something. Establish perhaps that she has a slightly murky past. Certainly murkier than his.

Girl explains it away by saying that it's only her parents' address.

Boy even more suspicious. Why has she written down her *parents'* address?

Her taxi fails to arrive – she decides to walk to the station.

She leaves.

The taxi arrives.

Boy resolves to follow her.

He takes the taxi.

End scene.

Note to self: explain in scene two how he catches the train, while she misses it.

Scene Two: the house, or perhaps the house exterior: less constricting than an interior and easier to lose characters who aren't needed in certain scenes – they can either go into the house or wander off to other parts of the garden. That's the good thing about gardens. People just wander without much need to explain their actions. This plot was going to require quite a dextrous shuffling of characters.

Note: it's a fine day.

And so on. This type of play requires intensely detailed plotting. It relies on coincidence, on things not being said or sometimes being said and misunderstood. Quite apart from the action itself, it requires that we know from second to second the attitude of each of the four characters to each other and what each perceives as being the situation. The wife, Sheila, for instance, will know practically nothing throughout. Greg will know a little. Ginny and Philip, the guilty parties, will know it all. And both will try desperately, in an uneasy alliance, to maintain the charade.

It seemed important, though, that by the end the tables would be turned.

Another decision was also being taken at this point, about time structure. The play could conveniently cover a tidy and brief span. Early morning through to early evening. Neat.

Ironically, when the play went to the West End in the so-called Swinging Sixties, I was asked to reset the first scene to the day before, around 4 p.m. – the argument being that audiences would be less shocked at seeing a young unmarried couple waking up together in the afternoon than in the early morning. I must say the logic in this somewhat confounded me. You mean they couldn't have been making love in the afternoon? I suppose it went along with the traditional student landlady notice, common at that time, 'No visitors in room after 10 o'clock'. So much for the traditional unities. I guess Aristotle hadn't reckoned with that one.

Anyway, the play, or at least the first half of it, was taking shape. But, please note, without a word of dialogue being written. I won't chronicle the rest of the plot decisions. If you want to read the end result then you'll need to buy a copy of *Relatively Speaking*. (Sorry, I promised I wouldn't do that.)

Essentially, though, with this type of 'clockwork' play – almost entirely plot-driven – once you've wound up the first act, the second act is to some extent easier as the spring is allowed to unwind again. Character in this instance is partly dictated by the requirements of the plot. Sheila, the wife, for instance, needed to be a vague, somewhat unworldly, apparently trusting woman – even if she was to get the last word. Greg, an innocent, impulsive young man – with a strong moral sense of right and wrong. Ginny, more difficult to establish, as she had to be sleeping around with older men and two-timing our young hero whilst still retaining our sympathy. Going to need an actress with a great deal of charm. (Charm is very difficult to write.)

Also, note to self: put her through it a bit as all her chickens come home to roost. The audience may then be prepared to forgive her if she is seen to suffer (just a little bit) for her misdemeanours.

Likewise with Philip, her ex-lover. Important to make him quite a sympathetic bumbler. (Though that's probably not how he sees himself.) Certainly not a suave, moustache-twirling seducer. He must also retain a certain sympathy – so also cause him a bit of angst.

Because of its very constructional artifice, *Relatively Speaking*, although always billed as a light comedy, is technically closer to farce – the hardest type of play to write. For some reason, at that time in the 1960s producers considered farce to be a little downmarket, so *Relatively* was accorded the light-comedy certificate.

With a farce obviously a good deal is to do with structure – making the improbable at least temporarily believable. Planting important information as casually and effortlessly as possible in order to close off what might be termed the corridor of coincidence. Yet at the same time, at the end of it all, trying to ensure that the audience doesn't tire of the dance, which will certainly happen if they either lose track of the plot or sympathy for the characters – in other words, if they no longer understand or care about the outcome.

No wonder they say that farce is an older dramatist's medium. The techniques involved are formidable. Only a youth of twenty-six would have the gall to attempt such a thing. These days, I know better.

The other idea, the 'theme' play, *Way Upstream,* which I was to tackle sixteen years later, was altogether different. No easy solution readily presented itself – neither time frame nor setting, nor even a set of characters.

In the end it was untypically location, the choice of setting, that presented the solution. I had spent a few slightly disastrous boating holidays with my two sons on the Norfolk Broads and the Thames. It had amused me at the time to see how the typical English male regards himself (often with no conceivable evidence whatsoever) as a true descendant of Nelson or Drake. I would watch overweight middle-aged men in yachting caps at the wheel of some rented craft, bellowing contradictory orders at their increasingly frustrated families. Of course, most of these weekend sea dogs, if truth be told, were within milliseconds of total panic as they tried to manoeuvre sideways through locks, wrestling with treacherous conflicting cross-currents that could sweep them over the nearby weir. Extraordinarily, despite this, these fathers and husbands still accepted their God-given right to be there at the helm.

Meanwhile, their luckless wives reluctantly resigned themselves to spending most of their precious holiday below decks, cooking and cleaning up after the 'crew'. No change there.

The problem of where to set the play, then, was solved at a stroke, and provided just the domestic scaling down to human level which I had been looking for. It also presented immense technical challenges, since I additionally resolved to make the play as naturalistic and real as possible, at least at the start. It seemed to me that the theme would ultimately open up of its own volition, taking on a more surreal form. The play would literally be a journey upstream, starting as a fable and finishing as a fantasy. When that change occurred, just as in the farce, I wanted the audience firmly on board with the characters and prepared to stay there.

As regards characters, working on the well-known law of minimum, I initially settled for five. The self-appointed skipper who was the 'natural leader' on dry land as well – perhaps the MD of a business. Let's call him Keith. The second male, Alistair, would be his partner, representing as it were the silent sleeping majority who, despite having access to similar power (he could equally well have been skipper), was prepared to leave it to others. Alistair's wife, Emma, would be the woman who'd drawn the short straw, the reluctant galley slave and dogsbody, secretly hoping that one day her husband might stand up for himself, for her, for anything. The fourth member, June, Keith's wife, would be the spoilt, rich dissenter, at odds with her husband, the one who hated the whole idea of a boating holiday, who refused to lift a finger and would far sooner have stayed in a hotel. Finally, Mrs Hatfield, the PA to Keith the MD, to provide us with a link to the real world. We needed her. Events on the closed world of the boat had to be reflected in the offstage real world. Though as that real world recedes, so, as a character, would she.

So far so good, but of course, all I had so far was a situation waiting to happen.

What was needed now was to create the vacuum into which something, someone quite unpleasant, quite menacing could appear. A catalyst, something that would threaten and finally upend this increasingly fractious status quo. As Keith's level of incompetence regarding boats, business, his marriage, everything, becomes apparent, and as his partner, Alistair, still refused to take over command; as the wives, one reluctant, the other indifferent, refused to intervene or do anything; enter a new character who – initially through charm and sex appeal, later through sheer physical menace – takes over and starts to run things his way, deposing Keith, overwhelming Alistair and brutalising the women. Enter Vince.

A little later, a final character was added – Fleur. A sort of acolyte of Vince's, she could provide an interesting sexual threat to Alistair and Emma's relationship, whilst Vince dealt with Keith and June's.

From there on, character more or less drove plot. And once Vince and Fleur were on board, events spiralled away into a frightening parallel universe.

☞ *Obvious Rule No. 6*
There is no hard and fast rule as to which constructional element comes first.

No two plays are the same. As we have seen, *Relatively Speaking* in a sense was plot-driven, with the characters to some extent tailored to fit plot demands. *Way Upstream*, despite initial inspiration coming from its choice of setting, is really theme- and character-driven.

Up till now, though, we haven't yet written a word of either play. Nor should we. There are other important decisions to be made first.

Time This is an area that's rarely talked about as much as it should be, I find. To me it's one of the vital choices to be made in play construction.

Even leaving aside 'time plays' – those, say, by J. B. Priestley (*Time and The Conways, Dangerous Corner, I Have Been Here Before*, etc.) or my own expeditions into this genre (*Time of My Life, Communicating Doors, Henceforward . . .*, etc.) – every play needs to have a time decision made about it.

ELAPSED TIME

During a theatre performance there are two 'time streams' running simultaneously: *stage time* and *real* (theatre foyer) *time*. A play may, according to the front-of-house clock, run for two hours and twenty-five minutes with an interval, while on stage we may have witnessed action that has taken us through twenty-five years. The choice here is entirely the dramatist's. The question I always ask is: in how *short* a time can I hope to tell my story – both according to the foyer clock and on stage?

I find it dramatically more effective to condense the stage action where possible. To conduct events over the course of a single day or night concentrates the audience's mind far more than meandering through a few decades.

Often the choice is made automatically by the narrative. If you choose to tell a story about three generations of a family then you may need fifty years in which to set it: Scene Forty – The Present Day.

On occasion, though, it is possible for the time choice to affect the narrative. I later moved the opening scene of *Relatively Speaking*, the one in Ginny's flat, back to its original early-morning immorality – I never got any letters. The result greatly tightened the play. Events all took place in a single day: early morning in the flat, mid-morning travelling down and breakfast on the terrace, late morning the meeting, lunch with the four of them and then late afternoon, wind it all up. In a play like that, it helped a lot. Time, by passing that swiftly, helped lend credibility to the confusion. The characters apparently had less time to think about things, thus avoiding our question – why didn't she ask him that? A question we would probably have asked had it been set over four days.

In the case of *Way Upstream*, the time span follows the demands of the story. Interestingly, it starts more or less in real time, one day following another, but as events blur into unreality, so the clock hands become less and less apparent. Day or night, winter or summer – who knows any more? It all finishes up in a sort of Thames Valley equivalent of the Garden of Eden. (Earnest Professor: Do the initials of Alistair and Emma, then, have some sort of significance? Author: Pure coincidence, sorry.)

☞ *Obvious Rule No. 7*
Choice of time affects the viewpoint of the observer.

The more closely stage time equates to real (theatre foyer) time, the closer to the action we appear to get. In a play like *Absent Friends*, the two time streams are virtually synchronistic. The result is to give stage minutiae considerably greater significance. In that play, over the course of a tea party, the selection of a sandwich, the pouring of a cup of tea, the embarrassed silences as the conversation lapses, are brought sharply into focus.

Whereas with a play like *Joking Apart* – taking place over all of twelve years – events are seen from a greater distance, as we witness not just a tea party but whole lives unfold.

Neither play, however, says more or less than the other about the human condition. They just say them in different ways. We can sometimes learn just as much about a person over tea as we can knowing them for twelve years. Provided we know what to look for. Or are gently told what to look for.

Time, though, is an ingredient like the others, which sometimes leads and sometimes follows on logically from the demands of the plot – mostly the latter.

☞ *Obvious Rule No. 8*
Generally try not to mix time speeds in a single play. It is confusing to an audience and can lead to a form of travel sickness.

However, to paraphrase another Stephen Joseph-ism, once you know the rules, they are there to be broken. It's just better that you know first what you're breaking.

TIME PLAYS

In a play like *Time of My Life*, once the theme was established (always theme first) time dictated events very strongly. The theme of this play is essentially enjoying the moment. Living in the present, not the past or the future.

At the start a family is celebrating the mother's birthday. The older son, Glyn, and his wife Stephanie (recently separated but temporarily back together) join the younger son, Adam, and his latest partner, the eccentric and outspoken Maureen, in the family's favourite restaurant, to dine with their father and mother, Gerry and Laura.

The party breaks up rather unexpectedly when Maureen, who has nervously imbibed far too much during the course of the meal, is sick. For the rest of the evening, once their children have gone, Gerry and Laura remain on stage throughout, drinking for two hours at the empty table, either alone or with the restaurant's proprietor. Slowly we see their lives unwind, in real time. We learn of their relationship with their children, their feelings for each other. The silences that occur between them – silences which are filled by other scenes taking place – are real-time silences. Never before had I dared to have two people on stage together not saying a word to each other, sometimes for ten minutes or more.

During these silences, we follow Adam and Maureen not forwards but backwards in time, through a succession of scenes that take us to a time two months earlier, when they first met. We see, as the play progresses in a succession of receding scenes, how Maureen has been made more and more apprehensive about the first meeting she is to have with Adam's parents, the closer it gets. Adam is terrified that his mother, Laura, will find his latest girlfriend, a hairdresser, somehow 'unsuitable'. (She does.)

Alternating with this, we follow Glyn and Stephanie forward in time over two years. We learn the wider picture. How Gerry was actually killed later that same evening when he drove home far too drunk and came off the road. How the mother, Laura, has since become a merry widow, travelling the world and reclaiming her younger son, who is now a helpless mother's boy – no girlfriend, no real job. And of Glyn and Stephanie's final break up, following her breakdown and recovery. Of her subsequent new life with their children – fresh husband, fresh start.

Finally, back to the start, or minutes before the start. The family are all arriving at the restaurant for the birthday dinner. The play ends with Gerry making a toast to the future.

That is using time at its most complicated. Yet it both reflects a theme and serves the plot, so in this case I felt the time-juggling was quite justified. Used this way, time permitted varying angles to be 'shot' of a single moment in time: it allowed before, during and after to be seen in long shot, medium and close-up.

In this instance, a lot of other decisions were to follow on directly from this choice of time frame(s). A single restaurant setting and the use of one actor to play all the various waiters, including the proprietor himself, were just a few of them.

Communicating Doors, on the other hand, is a more traditional time-travel play. In a hotel room in the not-too-distant future, a prostitute, Poopay, fleeing for her life from a violent client, finds herself twenty years in her past. It transpires that she is now in a room inhabited by Ruella, a wife whom the aforesaid client had murdered, twenty years earlier. The race is on to stop it happening again, i.e. to change the course of time. And when it turns out that the client also murdered his first wife, Jessica, we need to travel back another twenty years to sort all that out.

Here again, theme very much dictated that we would need to play games with time. The theme after all was that of lives changed by different actions or series of choices. The conclusion? That yes, wouldn't it be wonderful sometimes to go back and undo something, or to put something right? But failing that, perhaps we ought to be a bit more careful occasionally about how we live *now*.

It's actually a play with a simple plot and a fairly simple message, made interesting by its complicated narrative structure brought about by the use of time.

Obvious Rule No. 9
If a play can be too simple, it can also be too complicated. If one element is particularly complicated, keep the rest of it simple.

TIME FRAME
By this I mean the starting and stopping points of the play.

It is very important to choose exactly when a play's narrative should begin. A general rule of thumb is to make it as late as possible in the narrative. The longer the initial exposition, the more restless an audience is likely to become. A great unspoken 'Get on with it!' forms in the air whilst characters on stage are telling each other for the third time that they are brothers. I will deal with a lot of this in the section below on Information.

Your choice of starting point will help immensely, though. Think of your story as a piece of thread. Where you cut in is the point at which the lights come up on Act One. Where you cut out will be your final curtain. (There might be a knot or two in the middle to denote the intervals, too).

There is a great temptation to want to start with the biggest imaginable bang. It's attractive and sometimes it works. The problem is that for the rest of the evening you may find yourself trying to top it. Whet their appetites, by all means, but don't overshadow yourself for the rest of the evening.

The best place to begin is at a point when your story is already up and running, but not so far advanced that you can't fill them in about what's already happened as you go.

As to the ending, I once coined a phrase (I think it was me) that tragedy was merely comedy interrupted. Or vice versa. Our lives go up and down like ships on the ocean, and as authors, we have the choice of ending on a peak or a trough. Or, more interestingly, of ending midway between the two – leaving the audience to conjecture: are the characters still on the way up or on their way down again?

Sometimes, happily, you can leave your characters in the sunshine. The endings of both *Way Upstream* and *Communicating Doors* are positive, whereas with *Just Between Ourselves* and *A Small Family Business* I chose the darker course. Sometimes you can tease, as with the ending of *GamePlan*. Indeed, this was a particularly interesting stopping point. I felt secretly that the characters were not going to get what they wanted and that the end result would be rather downbeat. On the other hand, I felt that the audience, because of what had gone before, would in this case really prefer a happy ending. Solution: to stop before the true ending is revealed, leaving everyone to supply their own.

Sometimes the ending, as with *Time of My Life*, is simply inevitable. We know it before we reach it. All the more important that the mode of travel, how you reach it, keeps the attention.

Personally, although I always know the general direction my play is heading, quite often I may not know precisely when it's going to stop till very late on in the writing. (Stopping's easier than starting!) A lot of that decision naturally rests on what has gone before.

Obvious Rule No. 10
Never 'cheat' an ending to achieve a short-term result.
Whatever your choice, make sure the ending treats your
characters honourably.

Having stuck with your characters truthfully from the start, never be tempted to sell them short in order to get a quick laugh or a tidy curtain. People may smile through the curtain call but by the time they're at the bus stop or the car park they're already beginning to wonder if that would *really* have happened. Allied to that:

Obvious Rule No. 11
Never sell your characters short in order to meet the
requirements of a gag or even the plot.

A man once approached me to tell me he thought he'd solved the problem of the ending of *Just Between Ourselves*. I looked a little puzzled since I never knew I'd had one. 'Vera gets up from her chair,' he hypothesised. 'She smashes the birthday cake in her mother-in-law's face, then goes into the garage, gets in her car, reverses it out into the road and leaves them all standing there, speechless.' I stared at him. He appeared perfectly serious. 'But could Vera have ever done that?' I asked. He looked puzzled. 'What's that got to do with it?' I gave up.

For one laugh and about another £10,000 on the budget, I would have sold my heroine totally short. I'd never have been able to look Vera in the eye again.

TIME PERCEPTION
Or how we, sitting there in real time, are somehow made to believe that the actors are existing on another timescale altogether. So that when X says to Y, 'Oh, look at the time, I've been here half an hour,' we don't all shout out, 'Oh no, you haven't!'

This is really a matter of instinct. When in doubt, make it slightly longer than you think, rather than shorter. It's not vitally important but it does cause a blip on the screen of credibility if you're not careful. The opening of *Absurd Person Singular* gets it about right, I've found, when Sidney and Jane anxiously await their important guests and he continually consults the invisible fourth-wall kitchen clock. A remorseless countdown is set in motion as the minutes tick by. But they're not *our* minutes. They're stage minutes.

Location Otherwise known as the set. Or lack of it.

As always, the decision about where to set your play can be made either immediately – once you have the theme, as in *Way Upstream* – or later. There is, again, no particular order. Many decisions are made simultaneously or come as a result of another. Sometimes the choice of setting can really make a play that was till then just 'interesting' into something quite striking. My decision to set a very early play of mine, *Standing Room Only*, on a bus in Shaftesbury Avenue was a case in point. Even if the play didn't quite work, it was the first one I ever sold to the West End, almost entirely due to the setting.

Other examples are *Man of the Moment*, with its swimming pool, and *House & Garden,* which actually uses two sets in two separate theatres performing one continuous synchronous play. And so on. A good choice of setting can lift things. Some plays are destined by their nature to remain in the sitting room or the back porch. Others – like *Absurd Person Singular* – never took flight in my mind until I consciously switched its original sitting-room location to the kitchen.

Some writers seem to think that location is a decision made jointly by the director and a designer and has little or nothing to do with them. Certainly, you should always leave the experts to get on with what they do best – the details – but it is your play, and if you want to see it remotely as you would want it then you have a very definite role to play in the choice of how and where your scenes take place.

My own particular preference, as ever, is to limit the number of settings to as few as possible. Unity of place is always very satisfying and economical, not just financially but dramatically. As with time, too much movement can result in audience travel sickness.

It can also slow things up dreadfully if a lot of scene shifting is entailed. *The Revengers' Comedies*, my lengthy multi-locational two-parter, had over twenty-nine scene changes during its four-and-a-half-hour running time. If each of these took even half a minute to complete, over the course of the evening we would be in for an additional fifteen minutes of scene shifting. Designer Roger Glossop swiftly came up with another solution: pieces on fast-moving stage trucks, often intercepting one another on stage and giving an effect of urgency and purpose to the narrative.

There are several paths down which a writer can go as regards choice of set.

THE BARE STAGE
Literally nothing at all, or just hand props and small pieces of furniture brought on by stagehands or the actors themselves. Lighting and sound often come into play quite a lot, to compensate for the lack of scenery and to help establish otherwise skeletal locations by implication.

This is a solution that will be made despite your wishes if you specify too many changes of location. The director will be looking to keep the show moving and will most likely resort to the simplest solution – unless the budget is huge, in which case offstage trucks, flying pieces and under-stage mechanisms can be used. But you'll have a producer fighting you to the wire to try and dissuade you from that. In most cases, if you've written a multi-locational play and you've also dreamt of a set where the props and furniture are real and the walls and doors are solid, forget it.

THE COMPOSITE SET

These do work occasionally: I employed them in *Bedroom Farce* and *Wildest Dreams*. However, *Bedroom Farce* was actually written that way only because Peter Hall had asked me to write something for the newly completed Lyttelton Theatre, and I could not for the life of me think how to fill that big wide stage. So I divided it into three and wrote a play set in three different bedrooms.

☞ *Obvious Rule No. 12*
Always try to have the audience looking at the same thing at the same moment. A well-designed set will assist this.

The problem with composite sets, if you're not careful, is that apart from dividing the stage, they also divide the audience. Especially if, like me, you write for the round or an open stage. Some of the audience will have one of the sets continually in their foreground. Therefore, if the stage contains three separate locations, say, those people will be watching two thirds of the action across the distance of another set. Moreover, they will tend, because it's in their foreground, to regard this set as being the most important one even when you don't. In addition, because of the demands of the play, this set closest to them may occasionally have characters not currently in use, sleeping, dreaming, relaxing, or generally frozen, trying to keep a low profile so as not to distract from the far scene that's in progress.

The result of this, as I say, is a divided audience: a defocusing of attention. For some reason, audiences always find anyone frozen or doing very little on stage

utterly riveting, despite the best efforts of the main pro-
tagonists who are giving their all in another part of the
stage.

THE ALL-PURPOSE SINGLE SET

We employed such a thing when my regular designer,
Roger Glossop, tackled the problem in the original in-the-
round production of *Comic Potential* at Scarborough.

Basically this was a series of general-purpose units
which transformed into other units – desks becoming
restaurant tables, hospital beds folding over to become
sofas, etc. It's quite a good solution and it also tends, if you
do have to have scene changes, to be more interesting for
an audience to watch.

Another solution, especially for the round, is to employ
a permanent set that relies for changes of location entirely
on light and sound, or props that the actors bring on.
Woman in Mind achieved this very successfully when it
was initially produced in Scarborough.

I had dreamt up a play that was essentially seen through
one woman's eyes. What she saw, the audience saw. What's
more, what she imagined she saw, so did we. The problem
was that her imagination, as we discover as the play goes
on, is unreliable. Lakes, houses, trees, all shift location.
Increasingly, too, her grasp of the real and the imagined
becomes shakier and shakier, till we become as confused as
she does as to what is real and what isn't.

I was actually breaking the golden rule of consistency:
positively trying to muddle and confuse the audience, so
that they could have some inkling of what it must be like
to lose all touch with reality, as Susan's delusions grow.

The point is that the swiftest, safest, cheapest way to
move lakes and trees is not to have them there at all.
Designer Adrian P. Smith devised a simple grass space
which would serve both as Susan's small cramped suburban vicarage garden, in which she lived, and as her

imagined stately home, covering hundreds of unseen acres. The rest was done with lighting and sound. The garden became dappled in leafy sunlight whenever the dream garden was mentioned; a sharper, flatter light denoted the mundane reality of the suburbs. Similarly, quadraphonic birdsong suggested centuries-old oak trees; a solitary sparrow and a distant drone of traffic told the other story. We were able to switch location in the blink of Susan's eye.

Incidentally, when we came to stage the London proscenium version this was far more difficult to achieve. Proscenium theatres generally make scenic statements whether they want to or not; the round makes none unless called upon to do so.

THE PERMANENT SINGLE SET

As I have indicated, though this cannot always be achieved, it is always my preferred choice. This isn't because I have a passion for writing totally naturalistic plays in detailed locations – 'Oh look, there's even dust on the mantelpiece!' – but because using a single location brings into play a lot of basic theatre-writing disciplines. If you only have the one set, then the characters have to come to you. Quite the reverse of what happens in film or television where the camera delights in following people elsewhere – anything, it often seems in film, to get out of the same location.

Stage is the reverse. Location, often a major contributor in films, is usually far less important. It is there like the lighting and sound to serve the play. The best sets are there to frame not the scenic designer's certificate of excellence, but the actors' performance of your play.

☞ *Obvious Rule No. 13*
Beware of competitive scenic designers, particularly those with a 'concept'.

Chances are the concept will be something they developed long before they read your play and now at last they have found somewhere to use it. Goodbye, play.

Generally, though, it is enough, given a sympathetic director and design team, to give simple but clear indications. Don't be afraid to set them problems that you yourself can't personally solve. Why should you be able to? – you're the writer. On the other hand, don't be disappointed if they come up with another, more practical solution when your stage direction clearly reads 'Edwin spontaneously combusts'.

Obvious Rule No. 14
At least fifty per cent of your play is going to be visual.

Choice of location is important, though, and it's important you exercise that choice yourself.

OUTDOORS OR INDOORS?
Don't forget this option. Personally, I love the outdoor choice whenever I can make it work. I've probably chosen it for a sizeable percentage of my plays. It allows characters a greater freedom of movement. It's the equivalent of having a room with an infinite number of doors: it enables them to come and go with far greater flexibility. They can wander on and off at will or march up the garden with a glint in their eye, as if off to do something. They can wander through with wheelbarrows and saunter around picking roses. Once outdoors, people generally get 'freed up'. They sit on the grass, lie flat out, make love together or tend to gaze into the distance a lot more, which allows them to deliver unselfconscious soliloquies. (It's always difficult to address your remarks to a sitting-room sideboard, but outdoors, what could be more natural than to address the horizon?)

And of course, you can have a lot of fun with the weather. Rain, real or imagined, is a great way to clear your set in one sweep of a stage direction, as in *House & Garden*. In *Joking Apart* and to a lesser extent *Just Between Ourselves*, the seasons have a great relevance to the piece itself, besides allowing us to experience the passing of time from winter through to autumn. And in *Sisterly Feelings* and *Way Upstream*, it is the great outdoors that helps to drive the play.

Mixing the two locations, inside and outside, can work, though it's scenically more difficult. In *Relatively Speaking*, the contrast between Ginny's small flat and Philip and Sheila's large house exterior and extensive garden works to the play's advantage. Similarly, the open-air setting of *Round and Round the Garden*, one of the three *Norman Conquests*, gives that play a certain wild, back-to-nature feeling (it certainly sets Norman off) which the other two plays, in the confines of the dining room and the living room, can't achieve. And with *House & Garden* the two locations make for two very contrasting plays; the same characters behave very differently depending on which set they're in.

LOCATION DICTATING EVENTS

Choice of location can greatly affect the mood and tone of the play. The rather seedy hotel committee room in *Ten Times Table* gave the play a very distinctive, neutral feel that a meeting in one of the committee member's homes, say, wouldn't have given.

Setting *Season's Greetings* in the hall of Neville and Belinda's home gave a sense of us being at a crossroads in their house, allowing me to have characters moving freely from one part of it to the other, often as if en route. Additionally, by having both the sitting room and the dining room only partially in view I could employ a 'now you see them, now you don't' effect, and achieve greater flexibility when it came to shuffling characters on and off. This was not, please note, a directorial decision, but very much a writing one.

In some cases the setting virtually dictates the directing. In *How the Other Half Loves* the superimposed composite set – half the sofa and half the dining table belong to one family, half to another – contributes enormously to the storytelling and, incidentally, brings about fifty per cent of the laughs. Similarly with *Taking Steps*, where three floors are all contained on the same level with the cast running up and down imaginary stairs. This is not a directorial conceit, but is actually written into the script – though I have heard of a production where they solemnly built all three floors and did it with conventional staging. Both plays, of course, grew out of my experience of working in the round.

Whilst *How the Other Half Loves* has transferred reasonably successfully to the proscenium, *Taking Steps* rarely has. Privately I believe both plays work infinitely better in the round, where the floor is in full view of everyone. They are, after all, plays about floor space and where the round is concerned, the floor is the equivalent of the backdrop: the floor seen by everyone is the area where the designers can make their strongest scenic statement.

What you see, then, is often as important as what you hear. The visual aspects are also the responsibility of the author, even though they may and indeed should be developed by the rest of the team.

And of course, let us not forget the biggest visual contributors of all, namely the actors. But more of them later. We've yet to start writing this thing.

Characters

Obviously these are not the last thing you think of. Indeed, to a certain extent I have dealt briefly with character choice in the section on Construction.

Characters in plays are there, when it boils down to it, to perform certain tasks: to further the plot whilst also informing us – directly or indirectly, through word and deed – of their individual thoughts and emotions. That's an oversimplification but it's not a bad place to start.

Bearing this in mind, this approach means that no one crops up in a play without a specific function, which is either directly related to the main plot or part of a sub-plot that somehow mirrors the main plot.

Obviously much about a character is expressed through the dialogue they speak. I shall be dealing with that in depth a little later. For now let's concentrate mainly on characters' functions.

☞ *Obvious Rule No. 15*
Remember that your characters are eventually going to be played by actors.

I know, but you'd be amazed how many dramatists appear to forget. They write unspeakable lines of interminable length, couched in language that no person would ever use, and manage to say everything at such length that the actor really has no room left to act. They've taken up so much time saying the dialogue, it's surely time to move on – at least to another scene, possibly even another play.

I do believe that playwrights should think of themselves in part as orchestral composers. Before you sit down to write a passage for the woodwind section, say, it's handy to know the octave range of a flute.

Good actors actually have very big octave ranges (not necessarily musical) and it's more a case in this instance of discovering what they potentially *can't* do, rather than what they can.

They can, for instance, say a lot with their faces, their body language and their silences – sometimes more eloquently than your words can. A slight gesture can speak volumes and replace acres of text. Leave actors space when you write to display these talents. Otherwise they'll have wasted all those hours of movement classes at drama

school. Discover how much they can do with a very few
words, providing always that there is a clear indication
within the scene as to their inner feelings and motives.

Explore counterpoint. In *Things We Do For Love*, for
instance, Barbara's attack on vegetarianism in front of
Hamish, who has just told her he is one, conceals a sexually driven aggression which manages to make us laugh and
inform us of her inner motives all at the same time.

Have a clear idea about the role of your characters
before you start. What purpose does this one fulfil? Is it
vital? Is it even important? Is he just the messenger here in
scene three to deliver information? Can you do without
him? Is there another function within your storyline which
this character can perform as well, to justify his presence?
I know that every time you cut a character you're doing an
actor out of a job. But looked at another way, if the character you've cut gives another role a more significant part
in the proceedings, you'll have a much happier company as
a result. (They'll never know it was originally planned to
have ten of them.)

Obvious Rule No. 16
Never include a character with no real function.

It's expensive and leads to unhappy actors asking plain-
tively why they're in the scene at all. And it's even more
expensive when you're forced to cut their character later
and pay them off during late rehearsals. But it's artistic
economy again which I'm mainly concerned with here. In
Time of My Life, having one actor playing four contrasting
waiters as well as the proprietor himself gave the play a
nice comic frisson, besides giving the multi-ethnic restaurant some sort of unity and coherence.

On the other hand, always be aware of who you *do* have
on stage. A lot of my own comedy, for instance, relies on
there being two totally separate actions going on simulta-

neously, both of which can in themselves be played perfectly seriously. It is the incongruity of these two actions that can lead to the comedy. There is no requirement for the actors to be consciously 'funny'. On the contrary, there's no quicker way to kill the comedy should they attempt to be. They can, in other words, afford to keep a firm grasp on the truth.

If you ever see an actor giving a scene of yours a helping hand with a bit of extra comic business, there can be one of three reasons for this: either the scene is badly written, or it has been misunderstood and misdirected, or it's being played by a poor or unconfident actor with no judgement.

The second act of *Absurd Person Singular* is only funny when the neglected Eva is genuinely hell-bent on suicide. Her efforts become increasingly desperate. It still remains that any one of these attempts could potentially kill her if she got it right. Running full pelt at a butcher's knife wedged in a drawer is still a dangerous occupation. Similarly, the other characters – Sidney, Jane, Ronald and Marion – are only funny when they are doing their serious level best to help her with what they perceive as domestic chores.

A stage play, unlike TV or film, relies often on multiplicity of reaction. The camera necessarily tends to pre-select your view of proceedings. This preordained choice means that in general, when writing for those media, you should always indicate where the ball should be, as it were, at every moment throughout the scene.

In a play like *Relatively Speaking*, the four characters are often on stage together when all are at complete cross purposes. We the audience can actually take this in at a glance. Our eye moves faster and has a far wider range of vision than the average camera shot. Although the TV version of *Relatively* included some marvellous performances, coming as it did largely from the stage show, one always missed more than one saw, as the director and vision mixer struggled vainly to keep up with the characters' inter-reactions.

Obvious Rule No. 17
Never underestimate your audience.

You can afford to be subtle, far subtler than you think. They see and hear much more than you imagine. Most of them pick up most things – always provided your actors and director know their stuff. Well, you're doomed anyway if they don't.

Be careful just when in the storyline you introduce your characters. You can start with them all at once – as I did in *Time of My Life*, with all seven of the cast on at once. But normally it pays to drop them in selectively, if you don't want your audience to spend the first fifteen minutes with their heads in the programme trying to sort out who's who.

Ideally, they shouldn't need to have bought a programme anyway. Apart from telling you the real names of the actors involved, a programme is there to enhance a play, not to explain it. I always detect a certain lack of confidence when I open one which contains a glossary or a detailed explanation. If essential information is not in the play itself, we're in a certain amount of trouble.

I once saw a production of Kaufman and Hart's *The Man Who Came to Dinner* where it was felt necessary to print in the programme the biographies not just of the actors, but also the people of whom the characters in the play were originally parodies. Many of these originals had long since been forgotten, sadly: few people will split their sides at a witty parody of Hedda Hopper any more. Better to forget all that and try to make the play work on another level.

Anyway, most people only read the programme in bed afterwards – 'So that's who he was meant to be. I see.'

Obvious Rule No. 18
Let them know who everyone is.

Try and include their name early. 'Hello, Jenny!' is helpful. Or 'Mr Ambassador, how good of you to come,' does the trick as well. Give them as little excuse as possible to look down. Certain critics are past masters at this. Indeed some, I swear, rarely look up at the stage at all. And when they do, it's with a sort of amazement at who's now gathered on stage whilst they've been writing: 'Who's this Iago everyone's talking about?' No wonder they frequently get the plot wrong in their reviews: 'I felt the smothering of Iago's wife by Othello to be thoroughly unconvincing.'

Plan carefully each character's attitude to each other – loving, hateful, indifferent. Remember our manner and behaviour on occasion tends to alter considerably depending on who we're with. Observe certain fully grown people, for instance, confronted by their parents and mentally and emotionally time-travelling back twenty years or more – as a result, of course, of the parents' attitude to them.

Consider these differences and prepare to reflect them in the dialogue and general attitude. Some characters will change physically as well.

☞ *Obvious Rule No. 19*
Don't let them go off without a reason.

Begin to think seriously about the overall movement of your characters. Plot their actions, preferably from start to finish.

In *Relatively Speaking*, again, by sending Greg in to help Sheila with the lunch, I left the way clear for the crucial scene between Ginny and Philip.

Obviously the more technical the play – farce is the worst – the more you need to plot movement. In life people really don't need a reason to leave the room. In plays they normally do if an audience is not going to start remarking on the coincidence. Therefore, 'I'm just going to have a look in my handbag in the other room for a moment' really won't do. Not at all.

Whereas in *Relatively Speaking*, Philip striding off up the garden having won the argument leaving a fuming Ginny alone for a second is fine. Especially when Greg returns to lay the table and throws her into utter confusion and panic. Carefully planned, but the coincidence is not apparent.

Obvious Rule No. 20
Don't bring them on without a reason.

Normally, it's good to know where people have been or are going. Uncle Bernard, offloading his puppet show in *Season's Greetings* throughout the main scene on stage, allows the sequence to be broken up occasionally as well as giving several of the characters a chance to express their own views about the nature of Bernard's forthcoming entertainment.

Characters who are on their way to somewhere else are very handy. They don't have to stay long – just as long as they're needed. And bringing them from somewhere definite with a spanner or a dishcloth performs the other valuable function of creating a world beyond the stage itself.

OFFSTAGE CHARACTERS

These serve really as a sort of perspective device. As with the small prop only more so, they add a certain third dimension, a feeling that however confined the action is on stage, there is a life going on beyond.

I remember once in a children's show – not one of mine, thank God – the Prince turning to the children and appealing for their help in finding the Princess. 'Where can she be, children?' he cried. 'In the dressing room,' came back the answer. A case of a play failing to catch the imagination and remaining stubbornly theatre-bound.

It is important to create that other life beyond. There are little tricks of direction which can help this, but the author can do a great deal to set this process in motion.

Obviously you can use too many offstage characters. An endless stream of names, none of which we are ever going to meet, is extremely irritating. But judged just right – like my own offstage characters in *Absurd Person Singular,* Dick and Lottie Potter – they can take on a life of their own. This appallingly hearty couple served to create the offstage Christmas Eve parties during Acts One and Two even though we, the audience, spent the entire evening with the onstage cast in the kitchens. In Act Three, the Potters' absence usefully served to explain the non-appearance of Ronald and Marion's two sons over Christmas – conveniently for the plot, they had taken them climbing abroad.

In *Absent Friends*, the invisible spirit of Colin's dead fiancée, Carol, hovers over proceedings for most of the afternoon, much to the distress of the squeamish John. In *Ten Times Table*, the non-appearance of Lawrence's wife Charlotte, keen amateur actress and tenth committee member, greatly strengthened what could have turned out to be a slightly stock character had she actually appeared.

BACKGROUND

Characters need an offstage life as well as an activity. Sometimes a job is central to their behaviour on stage. Jill Rillington, the ambitious TV journalist in *Man of the Moment*, is actually at work. It's important that Leslie Bainbridge in *Taking Steps* is a builder or that Tristram Watson is a solicitor's clerk. It's essential to the plot. Other times it's not as essential and a passing reference to their job will do. It's enough to know that Ginny once worked in Philip's office in *Relatively Speaking* – heaven knows where that office is or what he does.

Significantly, over the years, as women's situation has changed, more and more of my female characters have jobs. Back in the 1970s, when I wrote *Bedroom Farce*, it passed unremarked that none of the four women appeared to have any sort of job. Any play which chronicles its time will eventually be overtaken by changes, social or technological. (One phone call could have avoided the tragedy of Romeo and Juliet.) But if a play's worth its salt it'll survive through the psychological truth of its characters.

It makes sense though, job or no job, to imply some other life for people. Even if it's only hobbies. Small hints, back references can do wonders. Mark's dream of one day opening a fishing shop in *Taking Steps* says a lot about him as a person. John's obsession with buying things cheaply and unsuccessfully trying to fix them is very indicative of his character in *Absent Friends*, and is one of the reasons he's driving his young wife crazy. Gilbert, the postman in *Things We Do For Love*, is far more significantly a keen part-time charity worker and weekend painter.

Characters in plays that are set in an actual workplace can be interesting. A certain selectiveness is required, though. To introduce people into an area that requires extensive knowledge is dangerous. Explanation, especially between colleagues, is difficult. 'I'm just switching on the main reactor, Hawkins.' 'Yes I know you are, Higgins. I built it with you, remember?'

In cases like this it's a useful ploy to introduce a stranger. A good device, this, but only of course if you can justify the stranger for the remainder of the plot. Adam in *Comic Potential* served to introduce us (as swiftly as possible) to the intricacies of a futuristic television studio. He could comfortably ask questions that the others couldn't ask as to what they were all doing. And since the technicians who answered were fairly uncommunicative, it served to keep their answers terse and to the point.

DEVELOPMENT

☞ *Obvious Rule No. 21*
Your characters must undergo a journey, too. Not just the plot.

Few of us remain the same. Most change over years – or even weeks or, in some cases, days. Where possible, it is always good to allow an audience to witness those changes in character that occur as a result of events. Unless, that is, you have taken a deliberate decision to keep one character constant throughout.

In *Man of the Moment*, for instance, Douglas remains infuriatingly the same. Infuriating, that is, to most of the other characters. Whereas Vic in the same play alters quite dramatically, as he consumes more and more alcohol during the course of the day and his true aggressive self shows through. So does Jill, as she becomes increasingly frustrated by the calm unflappability of Douglas; and Trudy, Vic's unhappy wife, as she grows to view this man as her unlikely saviour and redeemer. All the major characters are radically altered as a result of that one unchanging catalyst, Douglas. The minor ones, like Sharon the nanny, are in turn altered by the changes that the major characters undergo. In the end, no one escapes the consequences of the ineffectual Douglas's visit.

It is important to have some sort of map in your head of just what sea changes many of your characters will undergo. Or, in the case of an unchanging one, what effect they will have on others.

Colin in *Absent Friends* is another one who remains devastatingly constant amidst the disintegrating lives of his friends. In *Absurd Person Singular*, as the Hopcrofts grow more powerful and confident the lives of the other four drop away in disarray. Only the offstage characters, the unbearably hearty Dick and Lottie, remain seemingly unchanged.

Understandably, it depends to some extent on your chosen

timescale how big or small those changes are likely to be. But even if it only takes place over the course of a single afternoon, it is a dangerously dull piece of drama when not a single character alters or journeys anywhere from start to finish.

Sometimes that journey is made physically by an avoidable set of circumstances: the beheading and reconstruction of the two heroines in *Body Language* for example. Barbara and Hamish's growing desire for each other in *Things We Do For Love*.

Or sometimes by decisions made by the people themselves. The most dramatic examples of these are the numerous multiple choices made by the characters in *Intimate Exchanges*. What they choose to do gives them a choice of sixteen vastly different endings!

But even in more conventionally structured pieces, there are cases such as Jack's decision to save his daughter from the juvenile courts in *A Small Family Business* or Sorrel Saxon's to try her hand at prostitution in *GamePlan*. Both these plays are driven by decisions, usually flawed ones.

Sometimes it can be a journey made entirely in the characters' own heads. In *Woman in Mind*, Susan makes no clear decisions, but is swept along by events, imaginary and real, made by both the fictitious and actual people who populate her twin universes. She is, in a sense, a woman no longer in control, but taken by the tide. Nonetheless the journey she makes from start to finish is enormous and tragic.

DIGGING DEEP

Obvious Rule No. 22
You can never know too much about your characters before you start.

Finally, never draw back from exploring your characters as thoroughly as possible. Even in the lightest play you should have peeled off a few layers. Indeed, you should do this *particularly* in the lightest play. Maybe that possible darkness you have discovered will only be hinted at. But you really do need to know as an author that it's there underneath. For, once you start the journey itself and begin to write, who knows what you'll require of your characters?

I have started plays in my time fairly sure of where a character was going, and have been quite amazed at what they've blurted out – well, I knew it was there but I never expected them to say it out loud.

Final countdown You should by now be approaching the moment when you can allow your characters to speak for themselves. In other words, you are on the verge of dialogue.

The structure should be in place. And a clear storyline – either storyboarded or securely mapped in your head. You should know by now – especially if you're new to it all – who is where at what point, who arrives when and who leaves in what order.

Your characters (with names!) should be assembled, with clear objectives and distinct roles to play in your drama. They should have clear feelings for and attitudes to each other (though these might alter during the action) and they should undergo some development of their own as a result of events.

They will either control their destiny – and therefore the plot – or be innocent victims, swept along by it. Whichever, there should be a clear potential for intellectual and emotional movement, unless you have positively chosen otherwise.

A time frame should also be decided. So too should the place where the interval break will occur in the narrative, assuming you are writing a two-act play. You should probably have a scene breakdown as well.

Location or locations should have been chosen: real, imaginary, stylised or none at all. Thought should be given as to whether these assist or hamper your narrative – complement or contradict it. Remember, an imaginative choice of location can sometimes supercharge a story and give it a real dynamic and originality that it otherwise lacks.

If you are very new to the process, a scene-by-scene, even moment-by-moment synopsis is a helpful pro forma. There is, of course, no requirement to stick rigidly to this once you're confidently under way, but if you do find yourself adrift or facing a brick wall, it is then possible to trace your steps back, page by painful page, to the point where you first strayed from the allotted path. I once reached a giddy page seventy whilst writing *Ten Times Table*, before acknowledging that I had become totally lost. My mistake, I discovered, had occurred on page seven, when I foolishly chose to leave the single location and take my characters out and about.

In all cases, when in doubt go back to the classical basics: unity of time and setting. As few characters as possible and as strong a narrative as possible. If someone asks you the story of your play and it takes as long for you to tell them (should you be foolish enough to do so) as it does to see the play, then you've got a lot happening. If you can reply, hand on heart, 'Nothing much,' then normally, unless you're Samuel Beckett, you're in all sorts of trouble.

Assuming the majority of these criteria are met, though, it is probably safe to proceed to the next phase: the further exploration of your characters through dialogue. This, for me, is the fun part, and the reward for all the previous hard work. But as my late grandmother used to say, don't start on the pudding till you've eaten the main course. Otherwise you'll be like an upholsterer trying to cover a piece of furniture which hasn't yet been designed, let alone built.

Obvious Rule No. 23
You can't spend too long on this first phase. It can take at least a year.

Dialogue Dialogue, put simply, is characters conveying information verbally – about themselves, about each other, about events.

Sometimes they do this directly: 'Good morning, I represent the Practical Brush Company.'

Sometimes, for reasons of their own, they hold back. Sometimes they dissemble or hint. Sometimes they just tell lies. An actor once went through a script and wrote down all the adjectives that were used about his character by other characters. It seemed to me a particularly pointless exercise but I humoured him. Why, he demanded, were many of the adjectives used to describe him contradictory? Because, I explained patiently, they were said by different people, or sometimes by the same person at different times. Some of the time they might not even be telling the truth. They may be buttering him up because they wanted something from him. They might be trying for some reason to put some distance between them.

But then certain actors, if they see an open front door, will always go round to the back of the house, find a ladder and climb in through an upstairs window. They get to the front hall eventually but must reckon the detour has done them good. The benefit is never particularly discernible though, I have to say.

English – a nightmare of imprecision for lawmakers and compilers of statute books – is a God-given, double-meaningful gift for dramatists. Most things we say to each other can be interpreted two, three or sometimes five ways. Our choice of words can betray class origin, attitude and mood.

In *Relatively Speaking*, Philip's first words to his wife Sheila (after an interminable breakfast-table silence) are, 'I can't say I'm very taken with this marmalade.' Which implies an awful lot. Not hostile exactly. Dry, aloof – slightly sarcastic. Dispassionate, even.

When the play was 'translated' later into American, the adapter tried to equate this line with a US equivalent:

'This marmalade's a freak-out.' Something, I felt, had been lost in translation.

Philip could equally have said:

a. I'm very much afraid I can't come to terms with this marmalade. Not at all I can't.

b. Where d'you buy this marmalade, then? Eh? Eh?

c. For heaven's sake, woman, this marmalade is completely and utterly inedible.

Each one of these would have given the actor some indication of character, attitude and class: *a.* is pedantic, picky and probably suburban middle class, *b.* is more aggressive, almost menacing, from lower down the social scale, *c.* is impatient, dominant, and well up the social ladder.

The choices are infinite and each one carries a different shade of meaning. English undertones set translators endless headaches, so I'm told, as they desperately search for linguistic equivalents from their own often more limited vocabulary. From the basic double entendre, through the pun, the veiled insult, the verbal slight, the smiling rebuke, English is a great language for dramatists.

Take this piece of prose as an example:

As Tony spoke, Mary cast her mind back to that distant day when she had entered the school 1,500 metres and been lapped three times by Elizabeth Burnett.

And see how it might be translated into dialogue form to dramatise Tony and Mary's characters a little:

She I feel the same being with you as I did when I ran in the school 1,500 metres.

He (*smugly*) Am I that hard to keep up with?

She No. It's not just that.

He (*intrigued*) What? What, then?

She Elizabeth Burnett – she was the school champion –

built like a gazelle – she lapped me three times. Three times, would you believe? The race was over but they made me keep running on my own for two whole laps. While the rest of the school cheered and jeered.

He How awful. What made you think of that now?

She I can't imagine, Tony. I really can't.

Even in that brief section we see that what is implied is every bit as strong as the blunt direct approach. It's also more likely to make us smile as we secretly acknowledge that what the conceited Tony is missing, we the audience are comprehending. We side with Mary.

DIALOGUE TO CONVEY INFORMATION
In the majority of plays, dialogue generally has to perform a triple function:
   1. To establish and develop character
   2. To set the plot running
   3. To include sufficient information to allow the above to happen.
   The success of a play's opening depends to some extent on how well information is planted. It needs to appear effortless. There's nothing less convincing than characters who spend the first ten minutes telling each other things they obviously must have known.
   The unconvincing exchange:

Her Hello, husband.

Him Hello, wife.

   can be slightly improved. For example:

Her You've put sugar in my tea, again.

Him Sorry.

Her Just how long have we been married?

Here's the opening section of *GamePlan*, which not only sets up a strong mother/daughter relationship, but also gently starts the plot rolling. It also tells us all we need to know initially.

Lynette, a woman in her early forties, is standing out on the balcony coughing and smoking a cigarette. Her daughter Sorrel comes out of the bedroom, still in her pyjamas. She sees Lynette and shakes her head in disbelief. She crosses to the window and opens it.

Sorrel (*in exasperation*) Mum, what do you think you're doing?

Lynette Oh, darling, I didn't wake you, did I?

Sorrel Will you put that cigarette out at once, please?

Lynette Oh, come on, this is only my first.

Sorrel I should hope so, it's only six o'clock.

Lynette I didn't mean to wake you, go back to bed.

Sorrel You promised me again last night that you'd stop.

Lynette I will. I'm going to. I can't stop just like that though, can I? I read somewhere that can be just as bad for you, stopping suddenly, as it is to carry on smoking forty a day.

Sorrel Where the hell did you read that?

Lynette You go back to bed.

Sorrel Have you had any tea?

Lynette I'm just making some.

Sorrel I'll do it. (*She moves to the kitchen.*) It's freezing out there, come in. You'll get pneumonia as well. Mothers! Who needs them?

51

Lynette (*coming back into the room*) I was trying not to wake you, that's all.

Sorrel (*starting to make them both tea*) If you don't want to wake me then don't stand out there coughing yourself to death outside my bedroom window.

Lynette This is the last one I'm having this morning.

Sorrel (*unimpressed*) Great.

Lynette I don't know why you don't go back to bed. You don't need to get up for another hour.

Sorrel I'll do some revision.

Lynette You were up until God knows when. What time did you come to bed?

Sorrel About two.

Lynette Sorrel, four hours sleep isn't enough.

Sorrel It's enough for you apparently.

Lynette I'm older, I don't need sleep. You'll collapse. What were you doing till two o'clock, anyway?

Sorrel Nothing. Just on the Internet, that's all.

Lynette Well, I hope it was nothing – you know . . .

Sorrel What?

Lynette You know. Like that.

Sorrel Oh, come on, mum. I'm sixteen, for God's sake. It was just a chat room, that's all.

    Sorrel brings the two mugs of tea to the table.

Sorrel Here you are.

Lynette Thanks. Chat rooms. I don't know what people find to talk about . . .

Lynette sits at the table with her mug. She takes a mirror from her bag and studies herself. Sorrel stands and watches her, sipping her own tea as she does so.

Sorrel I wouldn't bother, you look terrible.

Lynette Thank you.

She stares at herself without enthusiasm, jabs at her hair with her fingers and then gives up and puts away the mirror.

Sorrel Were you serious last night?

Lynette Mmm?

Sorrel Were you serious? About us having to move?

Lynette We can't afford to live here much longer, that's for sure.

Sorrel Where will we go?

Lynette We'll find somewhere.

Sorrel Where?

Lynette Somewhere less expensive than here. I don't know. Maybe even out of London.

Sorrel (*outraged*) Out of London?

Lynette Possibly. Property's much cheaper once you get –

Sorrel What about school?

Lynette Well, you may have to commute, I don't know –

Sorrel Commute? Where from, Birmingham?

Lynette Don't be silly. We all have to make sacrifices. That's the price we pay.

Sorrel All except Dad.

Lynette What?

Sorrel Hell of a lot of sacrifices he's made.

Lynette (*muted*) Don't start on that again.

Sorrel Sunning himself on some bloody beach with that woman.

Lynette Please, Sorrel, that's enough . . .

Sorrel I hope he gets skin cancer . . .

Lynette Sorrel!

Sorrel I hope they both do.

Lynette Don't say that, even as a joke.

Sorrel I'm not joking. I hate him. The bastard. I hate him for what he's done to us. To you.

Lynette We were probably both to blame, I don't know . . .

Sorrel (*outraged*) How can you both be to blame? How can you say that – ?

Lynette Alright, Sorrel! That will do!

Sorrel Our business folds, he does nothing, you nearly collapse with stress and he runs off with your partner. Terrific. Thanks so much, father.

   Lynette is crying softly.

Sorrel (*contritely*) Sorry.

Lynette I don't want you to get like this. Please promise me you won't get like this.

Sorrel How do you mean?

Lynette All – bitter and – vengeful. It's negative. It's pointless. All it hurts in the end is yourself.

Sorrel I'll try not to be. Just promise me one thing, though . . .

Lynette What?

Sorrel If you ever see me getting seriously involved with a man that you'll shoot me first.

Lynette I've told you. Forget all about Dad. We start again. You and me. New life. Fresh start.

Sorrel And you're not even trying to get money out of him?

Lynette We don't know where he is.

Sorrel Do you think he'll ever get in touch again?

Lynette I wouldn't. Maybe for you, he might. Maybe he'll want to see you again.

Sorrel Me? He didn't even like me.

Lynette Oh, yes he did.

Sorrel Anyway, he owes us something.

Lynette He hasn't got any money, either. We lost the lot, didn't we?

Sorrel It was so quick.

Lynette These things are. One minute you've – millions. On paper, anyway – well, not even on paper – on screen. And the next minute . . .

Sorrel Bloody dead loss dot com. Dot utter disaster com.

Lynette We weren't the only ones. And there'll be lots more.

Pause.

Lynette I'm sorry I shouted at you last night. I was just tired.

Lynette coughs and by reflex reaches into her bag for another cigarette.

Sorrel (*a warning*) No . . .

Lynette Oh, come on! This is only my sec –

Sorrel (*fiercely*) NO!

Lynette hesitates.

Sorrel Mum, if you light that cigarette, I warn you I will, I really will walk out and I swear I won't come back. I refuse to sit around here and watch you slowly kill yourself, OK?

Lynette has another small coughing fit but puts away the cigarette, reluctantly.

Sorrel Oh, what's the point? You'll light up as soon as you're out the front door, won't you?

Lynette No, I won't. I can be strong-willed if I want to be. (*Looking at her watch*) I'd better go.

Sorrel Seriously. What are we going to do? We can't carry on like this.

Lynette We'll manage.

Sorrel We are clearly not though, are we? We're going to have to move, we've got no money. You haven't even got a proper job. I may finish up moving schools, God knows where we'll go –

Lynette I've told you, you are not moving schools.

Sorrel It may come to that, mightn't it? We certainly can't afford to live round here any more.

Lynette And I have got a proper job.

Sorrel What? Temporary office cleaner . . .?

Lynette It's a perfectly good job. Hundreds of people –

Sorrel Working twelve hours a day?

Lynette Nonsense. Dozens of –

Sorrel Getting paid next to nothing?

Lynette Sorrel, don't be such a snob. It's a perfectly decent job. Lots of people do it!

Sorrel Mum, you used to run offices, now you're cleaning them.

Lynette Times change, don't they? (*Getting up*) I'll see you this evening.

Lynette gets her coat from the hallway and starts to put it on during the next.

Sorrel And you still won't let me help?

Lynette What do you mean?

Sorrel What I said last night. I'm perfectly prepared to try and get a job. Part-time. Help bring in some money –

Lynette Sorrel, we talked this to death –

Sorrel We shouted it to death. I could manage both, easily –

Lynette Forget it. You have wonderful prospects. You're not jeopardising those because of all this. Otherwise it'll all have been for nothing, don't you see? As far as I'm concerned, my life will have been for nothing. Pointless. You're all that matters to me now, Sorrel. And if you want me to be happy, darling, if you care for me in the least little bit then you will carry on with your life and fulfil all that promise. I will not let you throw it away now. Just because I made a stupid mistake, I refuse to allow it to affect you. That is not going to happen, do you hear me? So, please, let's not talk about it again.

Sorrel is silent.

Lynette See you later, then.

Sorrel Yeah. I love you.

Lynette (*coming and hugging her*) Love you too. Bye.

Sorrel Bye.

Lynette *opens the front door.*

Sorrel And if you love me in the least little bit, then please do not smoke!

Lynette (*as she goes, wearily*) Yeah, yeah, yeah . . .

☞ *Obvious Rule No. 24*
Information gleaned indirectly by an audience is far more effective.

Besides getting a good look at both women we also get an idea of the tension that's grown between them. We can hazard a guess that the calmness of Sorrel is probably a result of having such a volatile mother with enough emotional energy for both of them. Later we will see the result of Sorrel's attitude, her determination to keep control of herself (and life) at all costs. And the near-catastrophic results of this. We remain flies on the wall but we are granted a privileged glimpse as they unwittingly reveal themselves to us.

☞ *Obvious Rule No. 25*
Important information should always be conveyed at least twice.

All the salient facts in that Lynette / Sorrel exchange will be repeated shortly in a future scene, i.e. the father leaving, the business collapsing, the threat of their having to move home, of Sorrel having to change school, etc.

If it's important for the plot (and all that is) then don't risk some audience member unexpectedly coughing over it so that nobody hears.

Here's another example of information 'salting'. Early on in *Woman in Mind* we are invited to side with Susan, the vicar's wife, as we see her for the first time with her infuriatingly complacent husband Gerald.

Susan is seated in a garden chair. Gerald is standing nearby. It is he, apparently, who has woken her.

Gerald Were you asleep?

Susan (*shaking herself awake*) I must have – must have dozed off . . .

Gerald It's eleven-thirty. I thought you should know.

Susan Why?

Gerald Rick's here for lunch.

Susan Yes, I know. You told me.

Gerald paces round the garden rather restlessly.

Gerald There is a school of thought that believes that sleep is for the night. You seem to be out to disprove them . . . Is that bush dead? It looks dead from here.

Susan I'd sleep at night if I could. I'm finding it very difficult recently . . .

Gerald Hardly surprising. If you sleep all day.

Susan (*rather irritably*) What do you want, Gerald? Do you want me to do something for you?

Gerald No, no. Don't stir yourself on my account. I was just taking a brief break from the book. Thought I'd see what you were doing. Now I know. Sleeping.

Susan Might I remind you, I only came out of hospital this morning.

Gerald Presumably they released you because they considered you fit and well. Anyway, Bill Windsor just phoned. Said he'd look in later.

Susan Oh, he doesn't have to bother . . .

Gerald Ask him for a tablet or something. To help you sleep. At night. Or perhaps a stimulant. To keep you awake. In the daytime.

Susan Has it ever occurred to you why I can't sleep at nights?

Gerald Insomnia?

Susan Perhaps it's because I'm not very happy, Gerald.

Gerald Well, who is? These days? Very few.

Susan You seem happy.

Gerald Do I? Maybe I'm just better at hiding these things. Who knows?

Susan At least you sleep at night.

Gerald Only because I'm exhausted from a full day's work. I give my body no option.

Susan Zonk.

Gerald I beg your pardon?

Susan You just zonk out.

Gerald I've no idea what that means. Zonk? There's your solution. Fill your day a little more. Then you'll sleep.

Susan (*flaring*) I work extremely hard, Gerald, and you know it. I help you whenever I'm able. I run this house for you –

Gerald With the help of my sister, you do –

Susan No, Gerald, *despite* Muriel's help, I run this house. I do all the cooking, the bulk of the washing up, all the laundry – including Muriel's – I cope with the sheer boring slog of tidying up after both of you, day after day, I make the beds, I –

Gerald All right. All right, dear. We don't need the catalogue. All I am saying is – you still don't seem to have enough to do.

Susan No, you're absolutely right, Gerald. I don't. Not nearly enough. Not any more.

Gerald Something the matter?

Susan There must be. I don't know what my role is these days. I don't any longer know what I'm supposed to be doing. I used to be a wife. I used to be a mother. And I loved it. People said, 'Oh, don't you long to get out and do a proper job?' And I'd say, 'No thanks, this is a proper job, thank you. Mind your own business.' But now it isn't any more. The thrill has gone.

Gerald Oh, we're back on that, are we?

Susan 'Fraid so.

Gerald 'The trivial round, the common task, Will furnish all we need to ask . . .'

Susan Yes, it's usually about now that you come up with that invaluable piece of advice, Gerald. The point is it's not true. They don't. Furnish. All we need to ask. Not on their own. Whoever wrote it was talking through his hat. Anyway, how can you possibly believe anybody who rhymes 'road' with 'God' . . .

Gerald All one can say is that they're words that have provided comfort to several generations . . .

Susan Good-o.

Already from this opening section, we have learnt a good deal about them, their relationship and their respective characters. Susan, short-fused and obviously mentally troubled. A bundle of nerves. Gerald, calm and patient but infuriatingly sarcastic and unsympathetic. It is quite apparent that this conversation is nothing new to them even if it is to us.

Wound into all of that is the intimation of the unwelcome sister-in-law, Muriel, and their son Rick's impending arrival at lunchtime. Both of whom we have yet to meet. Also of Susan's recent release from hospital and the impending visit from the doctor, Bill.

☞ *Obvious Rule No. 26*
Punctuation can help delivery.

Note also the use of punctuation in the speeches. Sometimes the speeches are broken up (quite grammatically incorrectly) in order to give an indication to the actor of the preferred delivery:

Susan Yes, it's usually about now that you come up with that invaluable piece of advice, Gerald. The point is it's not true. They don't. Furnish. All we need to ask. Not on their own. Whoever wrote it was talking through his hat. Anyway, how can you possibly believe anybody who rhymes 'road' with 'God' . . .

Not huge pauses. Just stop points to help shape the speech. Suppose it had been written:

Susan Yes, it's usually about now that you come up with that invaluable piece of advice, Gerald. The point is it's not true, they don't furnish all we need to ask, not on their own, whoever wrote it was talking through his hat.

Anyway, how can you possibly believe anybody who rhymes 'road' with 'God' . . .

It actually puts quite a different slant on the speech. Try reading it out loud observing the full stops and you'll see what I mean. The second way gives Susan a fluency of speech which she seldom possesses. Her pattern is breaking up like her personality.

Gerald, in general, speaks in longer, more finished sentences. He is someone who tends to think before he speaks and does not anticipate interruption, as opposed to the impetuous Susan.

Gerald There is a school of thought that sleep is for the night. You seem to be out to disprove them . . .

or again:

Gerald Presumably they released you because they considered you fit and well.

Note too at the end of some lines the '. . .', indicating, in my case, a tailing off rather than an interruption.

Susan (*shaking herself awake*) I must have – must have dozed off . . .

Gerald It's eleven-thirty. I thought you should know.

And a little later:

Gerald 'The trivial round, the common task, Will furnish all we need to ask . . .'

Susan Yes, it's usually about now that you come up with that invaluable piece of advice, Gerald.

This suggests that Susan is momentarily resisting the temptation to come back at Gerald, but can't finally do so.

At other points, though, I employ the '–' at the end of speeches, which indicates positive interruption.

Susan (*flaring*) I work extremely hard, Gerald, and you know it. I help you whenever I'm able. I run this house for you –

Gerald With the help of my sister, you do –

Susan No, Gerald, *despite* Muriel's help, I run this house . . .

For a brief spell they meet head-on, raising the temperature of the scene briefly as well as accelerating the tempo. A dramatist can do a lot to help the actors (and the director) by making tempo changes like these. An evenly paced scene, be it fast or slow, if maintained for too long, leads to monotony and loss of attention from the listener.

☞ *Obvious Rule No. 27*
Avoid bracketed directions (when possible).

Finally, note the paucity of bracketed indications before the speeches. The two that there are in the scene are both before speeches of Susan's.

Susan (*rather irritably*) What do you want, Gerald? Do you want me to do something for you?

And later:

Susan (*flaring*) I work extremely hard, Gerald, and you know it. I help you whenever I'm able. I run this house for you –

On both occasions it seemed necessary to indicate to the actor at what level these should ideally be delivered. But

most actors, believe me, get rather irritated if these bracketed instructions appear before too many of their speeches.
Some of them become quite cussed and deliberately play
against them, for instance practically yelling anything
that's marked '(*softly*)'. There's a difference between an
author being helpful and one who tries to give their performance for them.

Similarly, be very wary of italics or underlinings, and
especially of CAPITAL LETTERS.

Obvious Rule No. 28
People in general are reluctant to reveal themselves.

We touch, towards the end of this section, on the cause of
Susan's dissatisfaction. It's initially a very light touch. It
needs to be: this is not a subject, after all, that the couple
normally discuss.

Susan . . . But now it isn't any more. The thrill has gone.

Gerald Oh, we're back on that, are we?

Susan 'Fraid so.

Just enough to alert the audience. Then we dance away, con-
versationally, to other matters. Had they both engaged in a
frank sexual discussion then and there, it would have entirely negated our belief in the relationship. The whole point is
that they *don't* discuss their non-existent sex life, of course.

We are most of us by nature secretive creatures. We guard
our inner selves carefully – even sometimes from those we
love. In making characters reveal themselves they must be
given a cause, a motive. The classic, slightly corny one is to
get them drunk. Otherwise, they probably open up through
desperation, or anger, or deliberately to hurt each other or,
most usually, because they've no idea they're doing it.

A few lines later the subject of their sex life re-emerges

though, much to Gerald's embarrassment. We appreciate how much sexual frustration is informing Susan's condition. A feeling of being unwanted. Shortly, we learn that it is also the source in her of a great deal of repressed guilt, which will explain the gradual darkening of her private fantasies. Here she deliberately raises the subject, primarily to discomfort Gerald.

Gerald But I can't be of help in your case?

Susan We've known each other rather a long time, haven't we?

Gerald Said by anyone else, that could have been interpreted as quite an affectionate remark. Spoken by you, it sounds like an appalling accusation.

Susan (*offhandedly*) Well, you know I don't love you any more, Gerald. You knew that.

Gerald Yes I knew that. (*He pauses.*) I don't think you've ever said it – quite so baldly as that before – but I got the message . . .

Also, although it's still very much from Susan's point of view, we get a merest glimpse of Gerald's own feeling of inadequacy.

Suddenly everything's changed. We have moved from what was evidently a routine sparring match between them, into what I call an area of 'privileged information'. That is to say, we are hearing things now that they have never said openly to each other. We're going in deep this time. Note how it starts with that speech marked 'offhandedly'. An important marking, that one. A casually unguarded remark that will start a bush fire. Gerald, for the first time, is clearly hurt, and for a moment the balance of sympathy swings towards the poor man. She knows this will hurt him. She means to hurt him.

Susan I'm still reasonably fond of you.

Gerald Yes?

Susan Most of the time. Well, don't look so glum. You don't love me either.

Gerald Yes, I do.

Susan Oh. Come on . . .

Gerald I do. At least, I'm not aware that my feelings towards you have altered that much –

Susan What? Not at all?

Gerald Not that I'm aware of –

Susan Oh, Gerald –

Gerald I still feel the same –

Susan We don't kiss – we hardly touch each other – we don't make love – we don't even share the same bed now. We sleep at different ends of the room –

Gerald That's just the sex you're talking about. That's just the sexual side –

Susan Well, of course it is –

Gerald There's more to it than that, surely?

Susan Not at the moment there isn't.

Gerald You mean the sex – sex – is the only thing that's mattered to you in our relationship?

Susan Of course not.

Gerald That's what you seem to be saying.

Susan What I'm saying is . . . All I'm saying is, that once that's gone – all that – it becomes important. Over-important, really. I mean before, when we – it was just something we did together. Like gardening. Only now I have to do it on my own as well. It was something we shared. A couple of times a week. Or whatever –

Gerald More than that. More than that.

Susan Yes. Whatever. The point is that then, everything else, the everyday bits, just ticked away nicely. But take that away, the really joyous part of us – and everything else rather loses its purpose. That's all.

The whole core of their relationship is revealed in this brief exchange. The gloves, momentarily at least, have been taken off.

CHARACTER REVELATION THROUGH DIALOGUE

Dialogue at its best reveals the soul of your character. Through what it says. Or doesn't say. And because of *how* it says it.

☞ *Obvious Rule No. 29*
Explore the unsaid. If it's clear enough the actor will say it for you.

Here's a woman, Vera in *Just Between Ourselves*, who has lost all her confidence. Notice how she repeats words, how she hesitates. How her punctuation is deliberately staggered.

Pam Was it your idea to sell the car?

Vera Er – yes. I think it was, yes. I mean, after all it was my car. Dennis bought it for me but it's mine.

Pam Didn't you use it then?

Vera No, not very much. I – well, if we're going anywhere I go with Dennis. So I go in his car.

68

Pam But you go out on your own occasionally?

Vera Not to speak of.

Pam Still, I'd have thought it would have been very useful. Shopping, things like that.

Vera Oh, no. It's quicker to walk really. And then there's the parking and all that. It's very bad these days trying to park. Dreadful. (*Slight pause*) And then, well really I found I didn't really enjoy driving really. I used to get so tense, you know. All the other traffic and, er, I didn't seem . . . well, I'm not a very good driver. Dennis always said I couldn't concentrate. He used to hate driving with me. I mean he didn't show it. He used to laugh about it but I knew he hated it really. And I just seemed to get worse and worse at it. So I gave up eventually. I think I'm a born pedestrian. That's what Dennis said. All thumbs, you know.

Obvious Rule No. 30
You are as you speak.

Obviously what Vera says is important; but almost as much is revealed in the way she says it. Notice the constant use of the word 'really', including, at one stage, a triple 'really' in the same sentence. When we first did it the actress pointed this out and asked whether she should cut a few. I asked her to live with them for a day or so longer. As she and Vera grew closer, she never mentioned it again, but rather came to treasure this verbal tic.

Overall in that speech, I think we are able to view the core of Vera and Dennis's relationship, although actually Vera has no idea how much she is giving away when she starts talking: about the way her husband has eroded her self-confidence, probably without even being aware he is doing so. What starts as a joke has become little short of cruelty.

Contrast this with Anthony from *The Revengers' Comedies*, a man with overweening self-confidence. Disregarding what he says, just notice the way in which he says it.

Henry You couldn't be more unpleasant if you tried –

Anthony Oh yes, I could be. I could be a lot more unpleasant than this if I tried, I warn you. I can be deeply, deeply unpleasant, chummy, if I choose to be – believe me, so far as you're concerned, at this moment in time, I'm being as charming as you're ever likely to know me, so I should make the best of it. Because I'm not going to be made a public laughing stock by some poncified townie with a hideous taste in suits coming down here and bonking my wife in my own chicken sheds, all right? Now bugger off. Is that loud and clear enough for you?

Long, measured, unhurried sentences. Naturally authoritative – interrupt him if you dare.

By contrast, there is Tristram Watson, the disastrously inarticulate junior solicitor in *Taking Steps*.

Tristram (*clearing his throat*) Yes. We have only to cheque the payment – of the – no – pay the chequement of the vendor – of the – sorry. Of the purchaser. Outstanding. (*He clears his throat.*)

Roland Pardon, I didn't quite . . .

Tristram Sorry. I've got the contractual finalisations – the finalised contractuals – rather, contracts – ready. So there should be no obvious . . . er . . . er . . . er . . . oh . . . er . . . constructions . . . er . . . obstructions. Right. To the payments and completion. Of it all. (*Pause*) Yes.

Roland (*after some thought*) Yes, I see. (*He studies Tristram.*) Excuse my asking but you're going onto this legal business full-time, are you?

Tristram Yes.

Roland Ah-ha.

Tristram I am. In it.

Roland Full-time?

Tristram Yes. Sorry, was there . . .?

Roland No, no. It's just that . . . er . . . well, if you don't
mind my saying so, yours doesn't immediately strike a
layman as what we generally think of as a legal brain.
Just a first impression.

Compare in that exchange the distinct (if somewhat
extreme) speech patterns of the two men. Ideally during a
conversation of more than a few lines, it should be possible
to recognise who is speaking, even with characters' names
covered up. It's certainly something to aim for, anyway. But
to achieve that, it is first essential to know what each of
their voices sounds like in your own head.

LONG SPEECHES
Long speeches are good ways to reveal the inner thoughts
and feelings of your characters – though having said that, few
people set out to make long speeches. The long speech usually emerges as a result of the other character failing to interrupt. Or in Vera's case, as a result of a character who feels
socially uneasy with silence. Generally she's talked down by
her husband or his mother, so she never gets much of a say
anyway. In this case, Pam's silence unnerves Vera sufficiently
and forces her into saying slightly more than she means.

Here's another example of a long speech, this time from
Things We Do For Love. In this case the character does set
out to tell the others something. But she switches her emotional course midway. In other words she says more than
she means to, again.

Barbara has had one or two glasses of sherry whilst she and her friend Nikki have been waiting for Hamish, Nikki's fiancé, to join them for dinner. On Hamish's overdue arrival a row threatens to break out between him and Barbara. Nikki, to cool things down, asks Barbara about her boss, Marcus. It proves to be the wrong question to ask Barbara in her current emotional, slightly drunken state.

Nikki Tell us about Marcus, Barbara.

Barbara Marcus? Why?

Nikki I mean, what does he do? I still don't know exactly what he does.

Barbara Marcus is a leading investment consultant. He's a senior partner in our firm. *The* senior partner. He travels a great deal all over the world to advise clients. I'm his assistant. I try and keep his diary up to date, which is impossible because he's always on the move and constantly changing his plans. Still that's the job. I also run his office on a day to day basis while he's away. And most of the time while he's there as well. Until last week I had my own assistant called Sandra who was absolutely brilliant, but then went and got herself pregnant and that was the end of that. I now have Devonia Hargreaves who may last until the end of next week if she's very, very lucky. What else can I tell you? Marcus is married, as I said. To Miriam. His second wife. She's younger than him and quite devastatingly beautiful. And he has three children, James, Emily and Katherine. Two from Miriam and James from his first wife. They're an extremely happy, friendly, outgoing family and they all live in this wonderful huge house near – (*She is starting to come apart*) – near – Godalming – I'm sorry – near Godalming. It has a swimming . . . pool . . . and . . . a . . . tennis . . . court . . . and a . . . Excuse me.

She runs into the kitchen. Nikki and Hamish stand somewhat bemused.

Notice here how her speech pattern starts quite concisely. Barbara is externally a calm, controlled woman, almost frosty on occasions. The first half-dozen sentences or so are well-balanced, unemotional statements of fact. It's only when she mentions her former assistant leaving 'having got herself pregnant' that we get the first hint of editorial comment. From then on in it's all steadily downhill. Her ill-concealed loathing of her new assistant, Devonia – young and apparently also very attractive (we learn later in the play that Marcus has taken a fancy to her) – leads to the fatal description of Marcus's private life. Poor Barbara's secret love for Marcus is a secret no longer.

Note, too, how much she *doesn't* say, which says so much more about her feelings than if she had said it.

This speech, placed where it is, serves two functions. Firstly, it shows Barbara's own volatile state. But also, importantly for the plot, it happens in front of Hamish who till then has had little time for Barbara. Now his curiosity is aroused. Witnessing this sudden display of tears and female vulnerability provokes an irresistible desire in him to get to know more about her.

Obvious Rule No. 31
Unlike in real life, practically everything that gets mentioned in a play has a relevance sooner or later.

This is not the first time we've heard about Marcus. He's a good example of an offstage character being used to shed more light on a central onstage one. Earlier in the play we get this exchange between the two women:

Nikki Don't you get lonely sometimes?

Barbara I have my work. I have Marcus to look after.

Nikki Oh, yes. The famous Marcus. Still the same boss then?

Barbara I suppose you could call him that. Technically. We're more of a team, really. The fact is, Marcus can't move without me. He says these days I actually get his thoughts just before he does. It's extraordinary.

Nikki How old is he?

Barbara (*airily*) Heavens, I don't know. Forty-five, fifty. I don't know. (*Slight pause*) I think he's forty-eight. Next April. The sixteenth. He's an Aries. Why?

Nikki Nothing.

Barbara Oh, don't be so corny, Nikki. For goodness' sake. He's got this beautiful young wife. He has Miriam. He has three children. He's got everything in the world he could possibly want –

Nikki And he has you looking after him at work. Lucky old him.

Barbara That's my job. Anyway. Enough of me.

Nikki, the less clever junior partner in the friendship, is intuitively the sharper, the more sexually streetwise of the two. She is desperately curious to know more of her best friend's supposedly non-existent love life. Nikki, who goes from one disastrous male relationship to the next, cannot believe that Barbara has never had one at all. Now she senses buried treasure when Barbara is trapped in a dilemma, between the pretence of not knowing Marcus's real age, and her professional pride, which insists that she knows not only his age but also the date of his birthday and his star sign. There's no reason why she shouldn't, as his assistant, know all this. It's the fact that she initially tries to conceal that she does which makes Nikki (and us) suspicious.

Nikki with her uncharacteristically simple 'Nothing' hopes to draw Barbara out further. But Barbara's personal intruder alarm is now sounding. She attempts to laugh it off. Nikki, again uncharacteristically, comes back at Barbara quite swiftly (note the '–' at the end of Barbara's speech). But it's too late. Barbara puts the shutters up and that's the end of that. For now anyway.

But because it's a play, we rather hope as an audience that that *won't* be the end of it, of course. We anticipate, since the topic has arisen, that it will be revisited. This isn't always the case – things can never be that tidy – but in general it's true.

It will be four days in stage time and two scenes later before we get the next mention of Marcus. The seed, though, has been planted. The audience has diligently stored it away and they are rewarded.

DIALOGUE WITH A PROP

Obvious Rule No. 32
A well-placed prop can speak volumes sometimes.

Sometimes, I find, an inanimate object can serve to trigger deeper, more meaningful events. Earlier in the same play, reference is made in passing to a set of home-made shelves on the wall of Barbara's flat.

Nikki . . . Oh, it's all so beautiful, Barbs.

Barbara (*off*) Thank you. You see those shelves out there? I put them up myself. I'm very proud of them.

Nikki What these? Brilliant.

Barbara (*off*) Gilbert says they're going to fall down any day but I put that down to pure male jealousy.

Nikki I didn't realise you were practical as well.

Later in the same scene, in Barbara's presence, Nikki points them out to her fiancé Hamish.

Nikki She's brilliant. She put those shelves up herself, darling.

Hamish Amazing. That's impressive. More than I could do.

In a later scene, when the mutual dislike surfaces between Hamish and Barbara, he refers to the shelves again, this time sarcastically.

Hamish I just can't get over those shelves of yours, Barbara. They're quite an amazing piece of engineering.

Barbara (*unsure of this compliment*) Thank you.

Hamish They practically defy gravity. Breathtaking. The Forth Bridge of shelf design.

> *Nikki laughs nervously.*

As you see, we're getting some good mileage out of these shelves. In the first reference we use them to establish a 'who-needs-men?' pride in Barbara regarding her DIY skills. In the second reference, we see Nikki using them to show off her friend to her fiancé. She so much wants them both to be friends, poor misguided girl. In the third Hamish uses them against Barbara. He's experienced, at first hand by now, her anti-male independence. He counters with a deliberate low blow aimed at her DIY pride. But of course, inevitably, all these references to the shelves will ultimately pay off.

In the penultimate scene of the play, Barbara and Hamish, now lovers, have broken the news to Nikki that she is no longer wanted. She leaves, a shattered woman, betrayed both by her fiancé and by her best friend. Barbara is appalled. She has never in her life caused such hurt and pain to another human being of whom she purported to be fond.

Uncharacteristically, it is now Barbara's turn to start to fall apart. First Hamish is sympathetic, but as Barbara begins to wallow self-indulgently in her puddle of self-pity, his patience begins to tire.

Dramatically, I needed a moment, an incident which would trigger the next stage of their volatile relationship. That would drive her from despair to sudden uncontrolled fury. I wanted to take this self-contained, slightly self-satisfied and superior woman right to the emotional edge. I was looking for a simple, single action which would signal the start of the real storm.

Nikki, before her abrupt, tearful departure, has brought her school scrapbook (another prop!) down to amuse Barbara. The scrapbook has lain forgotten on the sofa till now. The case of one prop leading us inexorably to another.

Barbara (*tearfully gazing at the scrapbook*) Look at her, here, bless her. All dressed up for her dancing class, her little dancing shoes . . .

Hamish Yes, OK. Sure.

Barbara She looks so happy . . .

Hamish Listen, can you hear what I'm saying, Barbara? If we let this go, this – thing between us – whatever it is – then all this'll have been for nothing. Don't you see? Nothing positive will have come out of it at all. And what sort of waste will that be?

Barbara Oh, God. Look. It's the junior debating society . . . All in their little . . .

Hamish (*losing it completely*) Look, leave the bloody book alone, will you?

He snatches the scrapbook from her and throws it across the room. It unfortunately hits Barbara's home-made shelving unit which collapses spectacularly, spilling the contents on to the floor.
  A stunned silence.

Barbara (*furiously*) How dare you? How dare you destroy my home? Get out! Go on, get out! (*She pushes him rather violently*) Get out of my home, you animal!

The collapsing shelves invariably caused great delight to the audience who had been expecting and secretly hoping that something like that would happen. But the anger the incident provoked on stage was always very real indeed. And the fight that followed as the two tore into each other was genuinely quite frightening.

Of course, all this was back-plotted. That is to say, the need for the shelf moment arrived during the play's first draft. The earlier references and build-up to the ultimate destruction were then woven into the previous fabric.

Happily, and it always is happily if the ideas are flowing well, this prop could satisfy a number of plot and character needs.

Similarly with the scrapbook. Nikki, in a misguided attempt to cheer up her friend, has dug out her old school album, filled with nostalgic memories of the two of them in happier times. The revelation of Hamish and Barbara's love affair will cause the book to drop from Nikki's shocked fingers.

Similarly, in *Relatively Speaking*, Philip, the husband, now convinced that his wife Sheila and Greg are lovers, chooses the indirect approach to express his fury – in this case not even with the prop itself, but merely with a reference to it.

Sheila . . . I thought we'd have a cosy little lunch out here, just the three of us.

Philip snorts.

Sheila Are you all right, dear? Not too sweet for you?

Philip bangs down his glass.

Sheila Philip!

Philip (*angrily, glaring at her*) I've mislaid the hoe. Do you know that?

Sheila Yes, dear. So you said.

Philip I had a feeling it was you who used it last.

Sheila Oh, no dear.

Philip begins to pace around the garden in increasingly agitated circles. They watch him.

Philip I hope you realise that my entire morning has been wasted? I might just as well have sat here reading the paper, or had a round of golf like I wanted to in the first place. I'd have been far better off. As it is, I've spent the whole morning searching for something that should have been put back in its proper place to begin with.

Sheila I'm so sorry.

Philip So you should be.

Sheila Why me?

Philip You had it last.

Sheila I did not dear. You are quite mistaken.

Philip (*bellowing*) You had it last. I distinctly remember.

Sheila (*shrilly*) No.

Greg (*lamely*) Perhaps it's in the shed.

Philip's decision to move the argument about infidelity to more neutral ground – he can't really face the fact that he has been cuckolded by a man more than twenty years his junior – leads to even greater confusion. Especially to the now quite mystified Greg. Why on earth are his future in-laws behaving so eccentrically?

This is also perhaps a good example of how the use of a largely silent onlooker can add a comic dimension to a scene. By simply being there, they turn a potentially serious scene into a comic one, but without the need for any of the actors to signal 'comedy' in any way.

☞ *Obvious Rule No. 33*
The best comedy springs from the utterly serious.

Offsetting a highly serious scene with something equally serious but, through unintentional contrast, creating something quite ludicrous, is always effective – provided the introduction of the incongruous is prepared for and not signalled too much in advance. In *Season's Greetings*, visiting novelist Clive has been invited to spend Christmas at the Bunkers by Rachel. Clive is asked to be Father Christmas for the children on Christmas Day. He comes downstairs in the full rig, feeling rather self-conscious, when he meets Rachel.

Clive Rachel . . .

Rachel Yes?

Clive Just a minute, please.

Rachel Listen, Clive, if you're going to say something of great importance to me, do you think you could possibly take that beard off?

There follows a scene, probably the most intimate, personal one that poor lonely Rachel will ever have with a member of the opposite sex, which she is forced to play opposite an absurd pot-bellied Santa wearing a hat with a bell on it. Again the scene is inherently serious. The slant makes it comic.

In *Taking Steps*, Mark reveals to his sister Elizabeth that recently he appears to be having a disconcerting effect on people.

Mark . . . That's always happening to me these days you know. I'm chatting away and people just seem to doze off. Happening more and more lately. Is it something to do with my tone of voice, do you think?

Later in the second act, Mark and Tristram discover Roland, whom they believe to have taken an overdose of sleeping tablets.

Tristram I'll be back in to . . . keep him awake.

Mark I will.

Tristram You must keep him awake. Talk to him.

Mark I will.

Inevitably Mark talks and Roland slumbers. In a sense, an effortless joke. No funny lines required, just a collision of natural forces.

COMEDY THROUGH CONTRAST
Sometimes, by running two potentially serious moments together, they can cancel each other out.

Obvious Rule No. 34
Two darks can make a light.

The next example is another from *Season's Greetings*. At dawn, Clive has been shot by Uncle Harvey who has mistaken him for a burglar. The others gather, alarmed, and cluster round the body, uncertain as to what to do. Suddenly Bernard, complete with his doctor's bag, enters. Till now he has been the self-confessed failure, the man who messed up his life and achieved nothing. Now, suddenly, comes his moment of glory. He examines the body whilst the others stand breathlessly waiting.

Rachel Well?

Bernard (*gravely*) I'm afraid this man is dead. (*A silence.*)

Neville Oh, dear heaven.

Belinda (*in a little squeak of anguish*) Oh.

    Rachel walks silently to the front door and looks out.

Bernard I'm sorry. (*He moves away.*)

    A silence. A moan from Clive.

Neville No, he's not, he's still alive.

Belinda He's still alive.

Rachel Oh, he's still alive.

Bernard (*standing alone in agony*) Dear God, what a failure. I can't even get that right. (*He sits on the bench, alone and ignored.*)

Again, there is nothing overtly 'comic' in any of these moments – a man believed to have been shot dead, two bereaved women, a failed doctor who misdiagnoses – but juxtapose them all in the same scene and the result is almost invariably a very funny scene. I say almost invariably because, once again, the comic result depends entirely on the seriousness of the sum of its parts. If the man's death doesn't seem convincing, the women's shock and grief is for a second unbelievable, or the doctor's despair less than total, then the whole thing collapses.

In that scene there is nothing that can remotely be termed a 'funny' line. The tragicomic result is actually achieved with a layered build-up of character and situation, which started way back in Act One. Earlier Bernard, the doctor, has made a dawn 'confession' to Rachel when he declares his inadequacies. Again more sad than funny, it points us gently to the inevitable conclusion that follows.

He starts by referring to his disastrous puppet show which he staged for the children the day before.

Bernard You know, it just occurred to me, maybe because it's so early in the morning. I really am a dreadful failure, you know.

Rachel Oh, no.

Bernard Yes. Really and truly.

Rachel Is it because of the show yesterday?

Bernard Maybe partly that. I mean, let's face it. The poor little blighters were utterly bored to tears, weren't they? I hate to say it but Harvey was right. Absolutely right. He has a thoroughly unpleasant way of putting things but he was right. I really mustn't do any more of them. Enough's enough.

Rachel Perhaps you could do something else.

Bernard No, no. You get out of touch with children, you see. If you don't have any yourself. Phyllis and I really should have had some but she's so weak physically, you see. Maybe I should have done something about that but I'm not a very good doctor either. I don't think I've killed anyone, mind you. Not to my knowledge. I hope not. But I honestly don't think I've cured many people either. Just left things very much as they were. Oh well.

Of course not all dialogue is concerned with the deepest recesses of the character's soul. There are times when it's used to spin bridges of confusion. When the truth is concealed by misunderstanding.

In *Relatively Speaking*, the first meeting between Sheila and the young man, Greg, is a good example of this. Greg, to Sheila's bemusement, suddenly turns up in the garden, determined to make an initial good first impression on what he believes is his possible future mother-in-law. Sheila is in actual fact the innocent wife of Philip who, far from being the father of Greg's girlfriend Ginny, is in fact her recent ex-lover. Greg is understandably nervous; Sheila is politely mystified, desperately racking her brains as to who this young intruder might be.

Greg (*after a tentative pause*) Hello.

Sheila (*startled*) Oh, hello there.

Greg Hello.

Sheila Are you – er . . .?

Greg I beg your pardon?

Sheila Were you wanting to see someone?

Greg Yes.

Sheila My husband?

Greg Not altogether.

Sheila Me?

Greg Partly.

Sheila Oh, well then.

Greg I did ring.

Sheila It doesn't work. (*She smiles.*) Won't you come in?

Greg Thanks.

He comes further on. Sheila remains standing.

Sheila Do sit down.

Greg Thanks. (*Sitting*) What a beautiful garden.

Sheila Yes, we're . . . fond of it . . .

Greg I had no idea it was going to be so nice. Beautiful.

Sheila Yes, it is nice, isn't it?

Greg Look at those dirty great delphiniums. They're huge. How do you get your delphiniums that size?

Sheila Oh, well . . . constant practice, really. My husband's green fingers.

Greg They're like hollyhocks.

Sheila Are you sure you mean delphiniums?

Greg Well, those things. Whatever they are.

Sheila Oh, they're lupins.

Greg Pretty good going, all the same.

Sheila Thank you.

Pause. She smiles a little uncertainly.

Greg This is the Willows, isn't it?

Sheila Yes.

Greg Lower Pendon?

Sheila Oh, yes.

Greg Bucks?

Sheila Yes, this is the Willows.

Greg Oh, good. I suddenly had the sneaking feeling I'd got the wrong house.

Sheila The Willows.

Greg That's the one.

Pause.

A little later Greg realises somewhat belatedly that the poor woman possibly doesn't have a clue who he is. He determines to remedy this and adds to the confusion. We enter that territory, dreaded by all Englishmen (and women), of meeting someone who very definitely appears to know you, whilst you in turn can't remember ever having met them in your life.

Greg Look, I know who you are. I'm Gregory.

Sheila Oh, yes.

Greg Greg.

Sheila Oh, Sheila. How do you do?

Greg How do you do?

Sheila Have you come far?

Greg From London.

Sheila By car?

Greg No, train. I caught the early one. Specially . . .

Sheila Specially. (*Sudden thought*) You didn't stop by for a glass of water, did you?

Greg No. Why?

Sheila It just crossed my mind. People do quite often.

Greg Really? It's not a spa, is it?

Sheila Where?

Greg Here.

Sheila Oh, no I don't think so. It may have been, but it's certainly not now. Mind you, I'm quite hopeless at history.

Greg Oh.

Sheila You haven't come all this way for nothing, have you?

Greg Why?

Sheila To take the waters. You weren't under the impression you could take the waters here, were you?

Greg No.

Sheila No.

Pauses. Greg is rather uneasy and so is she.

Greg I seem to have got here first.

Sheila First?

Greg Yes.

Sheila Are there more of you?

And so on. The plot slowly winding up like a spring. As with all this type of comedy, the plot depends on avoiding truths that would dispel misunderstanding, whilst simultaneously sailing as close to them as it dares to get. It's a peculiarly English procedure – at least let's say we lead the field. The Scandinavians and even the French have a try, but for sheer bloody-minded opaqueness we surely come top. English-English, of that era particularly, relied on a type of genteel politeness which today, admittedly, is probably less likely to occur. Americans always had trouble with the scene simply because sooner rather than later in their culture someone would have said, 'Who the hell are you?'

Obvious Rule No. 35
Tell them all they need to know.

Normally, with that type of confusion, it only works when the audience is let in on both sides of the misunderstanding. If they don't know what's going on they tend to sulk and shuffle. Though you can hold back a little provided they have some sort of warning.

In *A Chorus of Disapproval*, the innocent Guy has gone round to Fay and Ian's house for what he believes is a straightforward dinner party. In fact, what Ian and Fay have in mind is a spot of partner swapping. We've guessed that much.

But what none of us knows – Ian, Fay or the audience – is that Guy's partner, when she arrives, will be the seventy-year-old nurse of Guy's late wife. This isn't revealed till later in the scene. All we the audience can guess is that whoever Guy brings will be highly unsuitable as a wife-swap.

Initially Fay and Guy are alone. Fay swiftly comes to the nitty-gritty. Or what she assumes Guy will understand as the nitty-gritty.

Guy You look very nice.

Fay Thank you. So do you.

Guy (*straightening his tie*) Ah.

Fay Do you want to take that off?

Guy No, no. No. That's OK.

Fay I love men in ties.

Guy Oh, yes? (*Pause*) You'd like it in our office, then. It's full of them.

   Pause.

Fay Look I might as well say this early on. Then we can relax and enjoy ourselves. If there's anything you particularly like, or positively dislike, you will say, won't you?

Guy Oh, no, no. I'm not fussy, never have been. I take just what's put in front of me.

Fay I mean as far as I'm concerned, don't worry. I'm very easy. I don't think there's anything. Anything at all. Well, I suppose if it was excessively cruel or painful . . . I would draw the line.

Guy Oh, yes, yes. (*He considers.*) You mean like veal for instance.

Fay Veal.

Guy Veal, you know . . .

Fay No, I don't think I've tried that.

Guy You haven't?

Fay No. Something new. How exciting. I can't wait. How do you spell it?

Guy Er . . . V-E-A-L.

Fay You mean the same as the meat? What does it stand for?

Guy No idea.

Fay Very Exciting And Lascivious . . . (She laughs) No? Viciously Energetic And Lingering . . .

   They both laugh.

Guy Vomitmaking Especially At Lunchtime.

   Fay screams with laughter.

Again this relies on a certain politeness on Guy's part. And a certain one-track-mindedness on Fay's. We don't altogether cheat. The clue that they were talking about different things entirely is there for her to pick up on in Guy's response to her question:

Fay . . . If there's anything you particularly like, or positively dislike, you will say, won't you?

When he replies:

Guy Oh, no, no. I'm not fussy, never have been. I take just what's put in front of me.

she might have guessed. But because they're strangers and she is steering a rather circuitous path, it's apparent from her response that she's failed to hear the second half of Guy's reply. All she probably hears is his 'No, no . . .' Her next sentence is clearly a continuation of her previous thought.

Fay I mean as far as I'm concerned, don't worry. I'm very easy . . .

Obviously it is up to the actor to perfect the confusion, but the dialogue can do a lot to help.

DIALOGUE TO ASSIST PACE

☞ *Obvious Rule No. 36*
Good dialogue creates its own inbuilt pace and variety.

Obviously, short, sharp exchanges between characters tend to help speed things up.

In *The Revengers' Comedies*, for example, there is a section which goes:

Henry Well . . .
Karen This is Chelsea Bridge, isn't it?
Henry No, this is Albert Bridge.

Karen Albert Bridge?

Henry Yes.

Karen You sure?

Henry Positive.

Karen Sod it!

Henry What?

Karen Nothing.

This is going to push things along a lot more swiftly than an exchange of ten-sentence speeches. Sensibly, one mixes the two. Pace, any pace is only effective through variety.

But there are other ways an author can help. At some point in rehearsals there is invariably a cry from the director (usually it's the director) to speed things up. Pick up the cues and don't pause before every speech. It's a favourite habit of many actors and usually conceals either the fact that they're uncertain precisely what their cue *is*, or that they can't remember what they say next. But sometimes it's 'thoughtful' acting: I'm all for that in small doses, but not when the thought the character is busy forming in their mind has the rest of us hanging around impatiently waiting for them to speak.

As the admirable amateur director Dafydd says in *A Chorus of Disapproval*:

Dafydd . . . Linda, you stop pausing for so much breath.

Linda I have to breathe, don't I?

Bridget (*in an undertone*) Not necessarily . . .

Dafydd You can't take that long breathing onstage. You want to breathe deeply, you breathe offstage in your own time . . .

☞ *Obvious Rule No. 37*
An actor can only go as fast as the dialogue will allow
them.

The best time to think (and to breathe), as any good actor
will tell you, is whilst the other character is still speaking.
BUT – and this is where the dramatist comes in – the actor
can only legitimately do this if the word or phrase that trig-
gers their response is built in early enough in the speech.
   Therefore this dialogue:

She You have all the agility of a three-legged buffalo.

He Who are you calling a buffalo?

will require He to wait till the very end of her sentence
before replying. Which will cause him to pause, albeit
momentarily, between the speeches. Or, if pressured, to
develop some precognitive ability to hear the word before
it's spoken. Unconvincing. Like looking at the phone on
stage before it rings.
   On the other hand this:

She You remind me of a three-legged buffalo with your
lack of agility.

means that He can answer immediately with:

He Who are you calling a buffalo?

Alternatively you can make He respond initially to the
earlier part of the speech, allowing the hurtful buffalo
reference time to sink in:

She You have all the agility of a three-legged buffalo.

He Agility! You can talk. If anyone's a buffalo . . .

Either way, they can get a move on and legitimately satisfy an impatient director.

Overlap is an extreme form of this and the same rules apply. An actor can only truthfully interrupt with a response when they've been given a genuine reason.

Many playwrights these days use the sign '/' to denote the interruption point. It's quite useful.

She You're lazy, you're deceitful, you're fickle / you haven't a decent bone in your body.

He / I'm not listening to any more of this. I'm off. I'm leaving. / Last time I come round here.

She / Go then. See if I care!

It's a useful notation – I believe it was first invented by the dramatist Caryl Churchill. Personally, since I'm going to direct myself, I tend to wait till rehearsals to sort this out. Overlap's fine at times. But, used in excess, it can have the reverse effect and irritate audiences. After all, they can't be sure that what they can't hear isn't important, even if you are. Incidentally, it *is* sometimes possible to hear both sides, if one actor is delivering at a slightly slower rate than the other.

Dialogue, then, is a lot more than people just saying things to each other, or even expressing opinions. Through their manner of speech we learn just as much about the character as we do from what they're telling us.

Modern dialogue has the appearance of being naturalistic. But in truth it is a careful construction designed to appear naturalistic. It is nothing of the sort. For a start the balance of the words within a sentence are carefully weighted.

Consider an instance of this in the earlier example:

Roland No, no. It's just that . . . er . . . well, if you don't mind my saying so, yours doesn't immediately strike a layman as what we generally think of as a legal brain. Just a first impression.

The punchline (well, the key words), 'legal brain', is held back until the very last minute. The sub-clause, 'as what we generally think of', is in there to 'weight' the line.

We anticipate the sort of thing Roland might be about to say following Tristram's extraordinarily inarticulate display. But when he says it, it's all in the timing. The final phrase – 'Just a first impression' – is what I term a 'for nothing' line. It generally gets lost under the laugh you get on 'legal brain'. But by giving it to Roland it leaves him with control of the scene. If the audience is slow, he can choose to pause for a fraction. If they're fast he can throw it in and hand control over to the actor playing Tristram – who is then free in turn to come in with his own next line when it's clear to do so. And if by any chance the audience choose not to laugh at all on 'legal brain' then Roland can close down the potentially eggy moment by coming straight in with 'Just a first impression'.

If all that sounds as if I spend my life analysing every sentence of dialogue I've ever written in that manner, believe me I don't. It's an instinctive process for ninety-nine per cent of the time. You either feel it, or you don't.

Moreover it's one that need *never* be discussed with actors. They'd be rendered too self-conscious to say anything. Nonetheless, I am always flattered and relieved whenever an actor recognises that they're misquoting the written text – whenever they realise that there is a 'right' rhythm to a speech, a correct balance to a line. They're the ones I tend to work with again.

The dialogue process, for me anyway, takes very little time. Days rather than weeks. But then with all that preparatory work, it really shouldn't take too long.

There are invariably other 'passes' to be made through the script. Literally, passing back over it, searching for repetitions, unclear moments, overstatements or maybe excessively favouring one particular character's point of view.

Sometimes they can be major, requiring rewriting the whole play. This last nightmare occurs usually when the whole concept was wrong in the first place. Glitches in the script are generally swiftly fixable.

Obvious Rule No. 38
Don't be afraid to throw it all away.

Or as my late great agent Peggy Ramsay once said, 'If you believe you have talent then be generous with it.' Not profligate, you understand, but generous. I think she was referring to those dramatists who have just the one idea which they keep clutched to them like a long-dead child years after they should have buried it and started afresh.

Passing back through the script is an invaluable exercise and, even with the ones which need very little doing to them, there's always something that needs revision. Tiny pre-plants for things that are to happen later: for example, Barbara's shelves or Mark's tendency when talking to send people to sleep. Characters may well have developed their distinctive speech patterns gradually over the course of the play. Now is the time to go back and standardise the earlier pages.

Obvious Rule No. 39
Read it aloud if you can.

Sometimes I find it pays to read the script as if you were the actor – that is to say, concentrating on a single character

Tidying up

and keeping in that voice for the whole of that particular pass.

A few days away from the script occasionally helps, as well. The play tends to get more clearly in focus. If, like me, you are going to be directing it, you need to develop a certain objectivity fairly soon.

But my preference is never to sit and pick at it for too long. A play is a piece of live art, not literature. It is a blueprint to explore and develop. I need to move on; to put aside the author and prepare to become a director once again. It's time to share the play with others. Thank God for that. This isolation was killing me.

DIRECTING

Having completed the script, there is a brief window of maybe a few hours, when you are able to bask in the glow of achievement and before the doubts begin to crowd in.

I am singularly fortunate in that even before I've completed the play, I know not just whether it will be produced but when. Being the director of your own theatre does have its advantages. The downside is that there is no one much who's going to tell you if you've got the whole thing wrong. Self-criticism has therefore to be rigorously applied.

I'm aware, though, that this working method is fairly unusual and privileged. Few other writers can boast such a set-up. Therefore, maybe before I come round to how I work specifically, I should say a few things about directing in general. What the job entails, how to get started and how to survive. It's a peculiarly indefinable job, really. And therefore it's unsurprising that amongst the public at large and a number of critics, there's a certain misapprehension about what a director really does – or should do.

Ask any ten directors at random how they see their approach to this elusive job and you're likely to get ten different answers. Indeed, ask a hundred . . .

The only sure-fire thing to be said about directing is that the rules change not just from director to director, but from play to play, actor to actor, production to production.

Directing for me is largely the art of responding to the needs of others. Or, as my own personal mentor Stephen Joseph put it when I first started my career, directing is about creating an atmosphere in which others can create.

The celebrated director Tyrone Guthrie put it another way: Directing is about filling everyone with the desire to come back at ten o'clock tomorrow morning. Same thing, really.

A simple task, you might think. Make the tea and sit back. But take into account that the 'others' that you are assisting in their creation are actors, designers, technicians and the entire support team that goes to make up a stage production, and the task is put somewhat in proportion.

What then precisely *is* a director?

A sort of history I once observed that a bad actor can spoil a scene or at the very worst a production. A bad director can close your theatre.

A director is a comparatively recent phenomenon in theatre. A relative newcomer, really.

Ted Upton, the company manager on my first West End play, *Relatively Speaking*, once told me of his first experience as a young actor when he joined a distinguished actor-manager's company back in the early years of the last century. Ted was first given one of the infamous 'cue' scripts which had apparently been in use in Shakespeare's time. This, in Ted's case, was a slender document in which his lines and his lines alone were printed, along with the last few words of another actor's previous speech, giving him the cue to speak. A device surely guaranteed to keep small-part actors in their place since they consequently had no inkling as to what the play was about anyway. Mind you, it also kept them listening since they had no idea when their cue would come up, either.

On the first day of rehearsals, Ted was summoned on stage where he stood before the actor-manager who was seated (upstage of course) on a large prop throne. The great man then proceeded to read the young actor his part, once and once only, with all the inflexions, pauses and stresses that he expected Ted to use. The actor-manager literally gave Ted his performance in one reading. He was to remember it precisely, on pain of death. Ted's moves for the play, mostly involving facing upstage, would be given to him over the course of the brief rehearsal period by the stage manager. The cast didn't see the actor-manager again until the opening night: the leading part was read in by a stage manager during the rehearsal period.

The emergence of the director coincided (and perhaps this was no coincidence) with the technical development of modern theatre and the decline of the actor-manager. From being an industry with basically two crafts – acting and writing – theatre developed, thanks to all the new technology, into the multi-skilled industry it is today. It was impossible for one mere actor-manager to keep track of it.

Similarly with our increasing predilection for revivals of classics, someone was needed to interpret and translate these often dense and incomprehensible texts; literally to decipher for the actor what he was supposed to be saying and how on earth he was meant to say it. The age of the great classical 'guru' director had arrived.

Of course in reality, given a modern text and a company who know each other and each other's working methods, there is no more need to employ a director than ever there was. It is just that actors have grown used to a director being around, indeed to such an extent that we now have what is referred to as director's theatre. This might be to do, in part, with the marked decline in the number of permanent theatre companies. Directorless companies do rely on a great deal of long-term working familiarity between actors.

The rise of the director might also be a knock-on result of film and TV, both of which are most decidedly director-led media.

All in all, it would seem that directors are here to stay, for better or worse – although they remain for the most part the most maverick and elusive breed in a profession filled with mavericks.

How does one start as a director? Is there a right way to start? Answer, no. Directors come from all fields, from within theatre and outside it. There are, true, a number of trainee director schemes but many apply for these and few are chosen.

Some start their careers by begging established directors to allow them to sit in rehearsal as observers or to serve as assistants. Others are lucky enough to be accepted by our bigger producing houses such as the National or the RSC, where they become so-called staff directors. Some come straight from university. Some are ex-actors, some ex-stage managers. There is no established route.

The career ladder of directing has only one rung: one minute you are putting out a tentative first foot, the next . . . there you are in charge and responsible for the careers and lives of upwards of twenty people.

There is no sure way to tell a good director from a bad one – particularly not early on in their career. There are directors reaching the end of their working lives, come to that, who have never been any good but who have not starved for lack of work. An actor can audition and at least give an indication of talent – or want of it; a writer has a play to show you, a designer a portfolio. But a director? Precious little. A few reviews perhaps – 'a fine production', 'stunning effects', 'sparkling performances', 'a visual and verbal feast', 'crackling wit' . . . Impressive, yes. But couldn't that all be down to the actors, the designer, the lighting and sound designers, or even – dare one say it? – the writer?

Going to see a director's work (surely there can be no greater proof than that?) is no sure-fire test, either. I once saw a show which I felt had been brilliantly directed, only to discover afterwards from the cast that the director had walked out after week one of rehearsal and that they had had to struggle on, alone and directorless.

I experienced my own fair share of directors during my brief career as an actor. Some would turn up only at the final run-throughs and clasp their heads in their hands. Others would sit puzzled in the stalls, giving off the air of

someone who has unaccountably come to the wrong theatre; they would worriedly write reams of notes, none of
which they ever gave us. Others would arrive with a master plan and galvanise the rehearsal room on day one with
the promise of things to come. Alas, they were never to be
seen again.

Stephen Joseph, genius that he was, was not the world's
most encouraging director. He preferred, in final run-
throughs especially, to turn his attention to the far more
interesting task of redesigning the auditorium. Not just on
paper, you understand, but physically dismantling it and
reassembling it whilst we actors struggled to be heard
above the din of electric drills and power saws. There is
nothing more distracting for an actor, believe me, than to
be in the middle of his emotional all and be told to cop
hold of the other end of this a second.

Then, when all seemed lost, along would come a good
director who listened and encouraged and understood and
watched, and for all the world seemed to care whether the
performance you gave was good or bad.

There is one certain rule of thumb. A show will always
benefit from the attention of a good director. Performances
will bloom under their encouragement, a style will form
and unite the efforts of all concerned.

A bad director can reverse all that. Far preferable to having a bad director is to have no director at all. The worst
sin directors can commit in theatre is to place themselves
between an actor and the audience which that actor is trying to reach.

It is not surprising that over a period of time, experienced actors often form very poor opinions of directors
as a breed. Long tired of offering their own reputations
up as sacrifices on an altar of directorial incompetence,
they view directors, especially younger, untried ones,
with deep suspicion. The formidable Edith Evans, on the
first day of rehearsal, observed a young man sitting in the

stalls. 'Who is that?' she enquired. 'That's the director, Dame Edith.' 'Ah well, I dare say we'll find him something to do.'

Nonetheless, it is a role which carries an extraordinary power. If a director has it in them to build and encourage, they also have the potential, even inadvertently, to destroy. There is no actor living who is not vulnerable to criticism, no matter how much they pretend to the contrary. Somewhere inside them, a negative remark, some sarcastic jibe, will hit home and eat away at the most confident, experienced, seemingly unflappable performer.

A director's comments can cause problems without necessarily being negative or malicious. Few actors like to be told how brilliantly they are performing a particular piece of business, either. 'I just adore the way, Brian, when you tell her you love her, that you smooth your hair.' Don't be surprised if that business rapidly vanishes as Brian thereafter gets increasingly self-conscious about a small piece of spur-of-the-moment invention.

If you doubt this sensitivity, ask an actor to quote their worst reviews. Most can remember them by heart.

Let us assume though, for a moment, that you are a good director – or have the potential to be a good director. How do you set about getting a show to direct? How do you set about directing a show once you've been offered one? How do you tackle – tame and if necessary subdue – the various departments that go to make up the theatre? I have spoken briefly of the actors, but there are other departments. What are they?

The producer   In order of meeting, the first is probably the producer. The one who employs you – indeed, employs everyone. In the West End this will be an individual – a Michael Codron or a Duncan Weldon. In the subsidised theatre it will normally be the Artistic Director of that organisation, or occasionally the General Administrator. They are the ones who normally send you the script.

There are a variety of reasons why they may have done this. Perhaps some kind soul has suggested your name to them. The author perhaps? It always pays to keep in with authors. Or the producer may have seen something else you've done. A stunning student production on the Edinburgh Fringe, perhaps. Or they may even have mistaken you for someone else – it's not unheard of . . . Another, more invidious reason might be that you've been suggested by an actor. This could be dangerous. I will return to that.

Another possibility is that the play's been turned down by everyone else and has finally turned up on your doorstep. Listen out for the phrase, 'The moment I read this, you were the first person I thought of.' Does this square with the author's copyright date on the front of the script – 1985? Should the reading copy look quite so brown, coffee-stained and dog-eared? I was once reading a so-called first-offer script and was halfway through it when a polite rejection letter from another director fell out onto my lap.

Anyway, whatever route it took to reach you, there's this script on your doormat with a nice accompanying note saying they wondered if you'd be interested in directing this new play and they'd be grateful for an early reaction, etc.

Obvious Rule No. 40
Never say yes unless you're certain.

The first instinct of course is always to say yes, yes, yes, please without even reading it. Saying no might be a sure-fire guarantee of never getting a call from that producer again, mightn't it?

Beware. An ill-judged 'yes' will, I promise, almost invariably lead to trouble and distress. For the one quality that a director must start out with and retain throughout the job is confidence, an unclouded certainty as to the potential of the script. As the project proceeds and all around you are developing doubts of their own, it is to you they will turn to hold it together. When the author broods and threatens suicide, the actors panic, the designers waver and the stage management mutiny, they will all look to you for reassurance, seeking an assertion that their contributions are valid and worthy, that what they are contributing to is worth their effort. Moreover, none of them will blame you when they discover you have been lying to them. There will merely be a sort of admiration that in this world full of mirrors and deception, you, a mere director, have managed to maintain the pretence so convincingly and for so long.

If you have doubts about a project when you set out, believe me, that hairline crack in your confidence will grow into a ravine.

But if you have accepted the offer to do the play, the next step is to meet the producer. Producers vary. They're all very nice to start with, let's put it that way. Some remain so, even becoming good friends. Others sprout horns quite suddenly. They all like lunching and dining a lot. In the early days, commercial producers especially can prove a ready source of good food. Keep in with a commercial producer and you need never starve.

The first meeting is often encouraging. They have faith in the product, they have faith in you. We have a list of stars who are already very interested in the piece. Indeed a couple have already read the play. They have one or two ideas of their own concerning the script and are anxious to discuss it.

If that isn't already beginning to ring alarm bells in your head, then it should.

The following unspoken scenario is beginning to unfold . . .

The star has received the script and has decided that with a little work from a willing and untried author it will provide just the vehicle he/she needs to return to the stage after ten years in a successful TV soap. The phrase 'get back to some *real* acting' will be used a lot.

All that's required of the director is to organise the tea breaks and probably make the tea as well. In other words, a director in name only. Probably one that won't in the end stay the course till opening night but, what the hell, by then the star will be in full control anyway and might even benefit from a nice newsworthy paragraph to the effect that they have gallantly taken over the reins on the final furlong.

Someone may be setting you up as cannon fodder. In which case my advice is withdraw gracefully. If you don't, you alone will be the loser. ('Frightful show. I didn't think even X could possibly be that bad.' 'What do you expect? Had no director, did he, poor chap?')

But I rush ahead. On meeting your producer, try to ascertain what your real role is to be in all these events.

Obvious Rule No. 41
Come cheap if you have to. But don't come malleable.
They'll have you for breakfast.

A commercial producer will be regarding you as *a.* cheap and *b.* malleable. At best – for let's be charitable, too – they will also be hoping to have discovered a new talent, one exciting enough to kick a bit of life back into the jaded old West End or tired old musical-ridden Broadway.

If your producer is an artistic director of a subsidised company, on the other hand, they will have faintly different motives. Yes, your low cost will prove attractive but your inexperience could ruin their year's budget at one fell swoop if you fail to get things right and empty their theatre. If you get things very wrong, by the time the lifeboats are lowered the show will be up and limping and playing to six per cent capacity.

In all events, with both categories of producer, it pays to stress your absolute commitment to plain, simple, back-to-basics, low-cost theatre with a minimum of set and costumes. It gives delight to one and relief to the other.

If you are sent a play by an artistic director out of the blue, it will possibly be one that they commissioned at some stage, which they have now gone off but feel nonetheless the author is owed a production – and besides they'll have a hell of a job convincing their theatre board members why they've wasted money commissioning yet another script which hasn't been produced.

Fair enough. But remember that the author will probably still be assuming that the artistic director in person (as originally promised) will be directing their precious play. Be prepared for initial hostility, then, from an author who feels fobbed off at having their baby entrusted to a trainee nanny like you.

It is really up to you to sift through these motives before accepting the job. If it's new, try and find out the origins of the play. Has it been knocking around for ever?

☞ *Obvious Rule No. 42*
New plays rarely build reputations.

A word here about old versus new plays. Remember that as a general rule, if you want to carve your name as a director, never accept new plays. Stick to classics.

Unless, that is, you intend to take a new play or rather a series of new plays and render them stylistically identical, with a distinctive, immediately identifiable design and production concept that is unmistakably your own. In doing this you will, naturally, do a number of promising young authors a tremendous disservice – but what the hell, it's a tough world out there.

108

An unusual production of a classic, on the other hand – be it a *Wild Duck* in rubberwear or a *Duchess of Malfi* on the planet Venus – will unmistakably identify your production contribution. Known of course as a production *concept*. Besides, it does long-dead authors good to turn over in their graves occasionally.

Whereas a new play done loyally and sympathetically, whilst it will bring satisfaction and occasionally even gratitude from the author – a generally unappreciative and ungrateful breed – will probably bring very little of that much-needed critical acclaim to swell the pages of your CV.

For sadly, critics on the whole are no more capable of separating the role of the author from that of the director than anyone else is. Generally, they credit the author with too much and the director with too little. Unless, that is, the director is already a megastar. But then what director ever became a megastar on the strength of new plays? Vicious circle.

So if it's a classic you've been offered, your chance to shine is far greater. But beginners can't be choosers.

If it's a classic, of course, you won't need to face one of your sternest tests: meeting the author.

Authors come in various shapes. When they come at all, that is.

The author

There is the new young playwright. Unused to the whole process of entrusting their work to others, they are often suspicious and have strong preconceptions. And quite often – and this is the surprising thing – they are extraordinarily ignorant about the medium for which they are writing. I don't suggest they need to have an intimate working knowledge of the practicalities readily at their fingertips – though I usually suggest to them that if they want to continue as theatre playwrights they would do well to acquire one – but they often behave as if this is the first time they have ever set foot in the theatre at all. Like a stone-age man who has suddenly entered a busy branch of Dixons. This type must be treated with great caution and gently told that they have chosen a medium in which the written word is only the starting point and not the finish line.

Then there is the new *old* playwright. Far more difficult to deal with. They have probably nursed this script for twenty-five years and they're damned if you're going to mess it up for them when they've waited so long. Especially someone your age who wasn't even born when their harrowing play about World War Two was still raging, dammit.

Then there's the writer who thinks they've written much more than they have and tries constantly to point out that, though the character may *sound* as if he's only saying good morning, what in fact he's saying is, 'God until now my life has been screwed up but catching sight of you over there with the bright red hair and the green dress has changed my life for ever.'

Rarer is the writer with absolutely no confidence in what he's written at all. I worked with one such who sat through rehearsals shouting 'Rubbish' from time to time. This can bring its own set of problems. It is often difficult to maintain morale among the team.

☞ *Obvious Rule No. 43*
Beware of the writer–director.

A worst-case scenario is that you are unlucky enough to come up against the would-be or indeed, heaven forbid, established writer–director. In which case my advice would be to run, run, run. Just ask yourself these questions. Do you honestly believe they intend to sit quietly at the back during your rehearsal period and won't resist putting their directorial oar in? If they are directors, why the hell aren't they directing this thing themselves? Is there something about it they aren't quite sure about and that they're hoping that you will fix? Run.

If you find yourself faced with a living author who is experienced, then they will probably be regarding you with some wariness. It could well be, unless you are personal friends and they suggested you in the first place, that you are their tenth choice and they are still smarting from Richard Eyre or Michael Blakemore's lack of enthusiasm for their best play yet. In other words, someone has foisted you upon them.

Being experienced campaigners, at the first meeting they will usually attempt to get in first, to ensure that your view is their view. It would pay to listen and wherever possible to agree wholeheartedly. As regards the meaning of the play they will invariably know more. Occasionally they will think they've said more than they have. They will assume areas of apparent subtext where no inkling of such a thing is indicated. Nonetheless they will know their characters – it's worth hearing about them.

As regards interpretation, you may need to tread more warily. As I said earlier, many playwrights are not naturally theatre creatures – certainly they are rarely *visual* theatre creatures. I have seen them sit there and watch their play physically unfold with a look of total amazement, bordering sometimes on delight, sometimes on dismay. What was in their head has been made three-dimensional flesh.

Whatever happens, you must do your best to identify and iron out the differences between you long before you reach the rehearsal room. The sight of an author and a director engaged in pitched battle in mid-rehearsal has a curiously demoralising effect on the actors. It is they, after all, who are being asked to stay aboard this apparently sinking ship long after you two have punched holes in it and jumped ashore.

☞ *Obvious Rule No. 44*
Get the script right first.

Meet the author, then, and talk. Talk a lot. As much as it takes. But let it be known that you are the one who will be doing the talking during rehearsals. When an actor creeps behind your back (as they undoubtedly will), hoping for some first-hand help from the author, encourage the writer to say, 'I've no idea, ask the director.' Many of the problems – provided the script is basically sound, and if you don't think that then why the hell are you going ahead with it? – can be solved in advance. It helps to remember:

☞ *Obvious Rule No. 45*
All writers overwrite (including Shakespeare).

CUTTING

Cut in advance. And then have the whole script retyped. If you don't it will come back to haunt you later, I promise.

Actor: 'Of course, you see, I hate to say this, but I think the whole scene would work for me, if I was allowed to reinstate that lovely speech of John's that you cut. I mean it says everything about this man's inability to communicate. And what's it going to add to the running time? Half a minute?'

Ha! Ha! Ten minutes minimum at the speed he's playing the rest of it. Never give them the chance. Delete all evidence of an earlier version before it reaches the actors.

Similarly, cutting in rehearsal can also be a battle. An actor who has sat up late learning a speech, rehearsing it, shaping it, even getting laughs in rehearsal from his colleagues, is often reluctant to relinquish it. Especially if the cut is palpably to do with length rather than dramatic relevance. The better the job you're doing with the production, the more reluctant they'll be to do that. After all, in week one there you were telling him how important that speech was and how the way he was playing it set off the whole keynote for the evening, and here you are in week three cutting it simply because the whole play appears to be running three hours ten without an interval. Try and get the length right before you start.

Indeed, if the actor does accept such a cut with alacrity, be assured that they have already mentally written off the show as a likely disaster and are anxious to have as little to do with it as possible. Once, whilst I was still acting, in some clear catastrophe, I succeeded in reducing a voluble leading part down to a series of John Wayne-like monosyllables. Yep. Nope. Guess who got the reviews.

REWRITING SPEECHES

Try and get this done in advance, too. Constant alterations to a text in rehearsal can give an impression that everything is up for grabs. Soon the stage manager will be providing curtain lines and the technicians will be chipping in with some good additional visual gags. Technicians who spend a large amount of their time gazing at plays through glass and hearing the dialogue second-hand over indistinct tannoy speakers are very partial to visual gags.

It does no harm, without resorting to bland complacency, to arrive with the author on the first day of rehearsals looking as if you're reasonably satisfied with what you've got.

But even though you've got it right, the next four weeks or so will be about getting it right once more – only this time in the company of others.

In the distant future there will be another phase, known as getting it right once and for all. This is during public previews, or if you're very unlucky, the press night.

So you have a producer, a writer and you. What next? If the producer is a commercial one there may well have been some initial approach to a star or two.

Stars This may mean your meeting the star (with or without the author) either in the producer's office or some neutral venue, for a drink and/or perhaps a cosy meal. The producer and the star will have worked together happily some years ago, or if they haven't, they will pretend to have done. You will find little to contribute to their conversation, not knowing who the hell Ricky, Sam, Arnold or dearest Joanie are. Sit and smile but on no account drink too fast or too much. Remember, these people are used to handling it and you're not.

Right at the end of the meeting, ten minutes before the star has to leave for a costume fitting at Shepperton or Los Angeles, the conversation will swing round to the play. Practically nothing of any value will be said except that the star likes it – has certain misgivings about the end, the beginning and a few moments in the middle but nothing that can't be fixed.

This meeting may be repeated a number of times with different stars, all of whom end up saying no. It can be very frustrating.

What is a star, precisely? A star is a mixture of the following. Someone well known to the public, sometimes as a result of one performance, in a soap or a sitcom or over a series of plays in which they've played more or less identical characters. Sometimes they are famous for other things not remotely to do with the theatre or acting. A sports personality, a newsreader or a streaker who disrupted the Test match at Lord's.

☞ *Obvious Rule No. 46*
Never cast a celebrity.

Have nothing to do with these overnight one-minute wonders. They will tire of the magic of the theatre after three days, once they realise what hard work it is compared to sports, newsreading or streaking, and will become mysteriously indisposed.

Alternatively, a star can be someone who has grown slowly over the years into the public consciousness, as a result of a body of work. With the decline in the mass popularity of the theatre this is far more difficult to achieve. Even big theatre stars occasionally carry, in the tabloid press at least, the byline from some film or TV series. Whereas even a few years earlier one would never have dreamt of billing Laurence (*Richard III*) Olivier.

Obvious Rule No. 47
Every star brings baggage.

Stars are actors who have a particular personal relationship with their public. Their fans come to see them and not primarily the play. Indeed, some of these fans may never have been to a theatre before at all. It's a good feeling to think that this will introduce a fresh audience to the theatre. But in my experience, most of them will never enter a theatre again.

This personal following has two implications, as far as you're concerned. Firstly, the star will demand a far greater input into what you are doing to their carefully created image than the normal actor will. Secondly, they will quite understandably not normally want that image altered or tampered with.

Even if they do, beware. For the other side of that equation is that their public certainly won't want that image to change, even if the star does. They will not want to see their favourite comic-soap henpecked husband transformed into a snarling wife beater. That is not their idea of value for money.

All this is not necessarily the star's fault, but simply the cross of fame they have to bear. As a general rule, though, however talented a star is, make sure they're playing more or less what their public expects them to be playing. Robert Morley once said that all he required from other

members of the cast was for them all to stand round looking at him adoringly. That's what his public expected and
he wasn't having people arguing on stage in any play he
was in, so there.

If a star wants to break their mould, and probably along
with it the link with their public, let them do it in someone
else's play. If they fail to deliver that old familiar magic for
which they are famous it will be you and the author who'll
be blamed.

The other distinguishing characteristic of a star is the
interest they take in other departments. Many stars have
strong views on costume, wigs, sets and lighting (especially lighting). They have a well-developed sense of their
image. Some are seen to be pacing the stage early in the
morning in earnest consultation with the lighting designer.
'It seems a trifle gloomy over there, John. Would you be
terribly sweet and just show me the state. I need to see the
lighting state. I know, I know, it's me but I'm having terrible problems finding any light at all. And it's such a key
moment for me . . .'

Personally, I've never subscribed to the theory that the
only way one can get laughs is with all the lights on at full,
but try telling that to a star. If you want them to think
they've got enough light, incidentally, and don't want to
compromise the visual effect, a good tip is to persuade the
lighting designer to make everything darker one second
before the star's entrance. As soon as they enter, bump the
lights back to normal. Unless they are carrying a light
meter (though I swear some of them do) that usually serves
to shut them up.

Stars are also interested in publicity, scenes other than
their own and other people's performances. Be prepared to
trade off some of this. There are some areas where this
interest can be harmless, even beneficial. They probably
know, for instance, what clothes suit them and even a bit
about how they light best. Other people's performances are

a dubious area and comments should be discouraged even when made for the most altruistic reasons. At best, the other actor will be receiving two sets of information – your notes and the star's notes. This can cause confusion and unhappiness.

As I say, a trade-off is sometimes necessary. I once allowed a star to come on stage at the half every night and reset the props, in exchange for not redirecting whole scenes they weren't even in. We got through several tearful ASMs but at least the play survived. It's a tough business.

Obvious Rule No. 48
Stars eat authors for breakfast.

Most important, try and protect the new author from the star. If the author is to be likened to a lost dog in Kansas then the star is the Wicked Witch of the East. It is your job to serve as the good fairy and guide the author's feet safely along the yellow brick road.

Popular legend has it that actors are vain creatures. Some are, some aren't. Authors, though, poor lonely people, are nine tenths vanity; they live their whole lives believing without question all the good things that have ever been written about them. Stars, meanwhile, have practised honeyed tongues. An author is therefore putty in their hands. I once overheard a star in conversation with an author en route by train from London to Glasgow. By York she had utterly changed the play. In her favour. Most distressingly, the author was convinced it was his own idea.

However, I digress.

Around this time, the rest of your creative team will begin to be assembled. This will normally be done in consultation with your producer. The creative team are the experts there to help and assist you with your production. They are all (unless you're very unlucky) experts in their own field: set design, costume, lighting, sound, etc. But in every case, ultimately they're only as good as the brief you give to them.

Directing is about talking and talking early. Avoid the temptation to be mysterious. Let them into your thinking. If you don't carry them with you, later you may find, inadvertently or not, that they are lined up against you; they will begin to sense that due to no clear brief – or worse, to a constantly changing brief – their own professional reputations are at stake.

Set designers   In commercial theatre, there will be a whole field to chose from. If, on the other hand, you're dealing with a regional company, they may well employ resident in-house designers they would prefer you to use. Whichever, it's important you have approval of these. Don't let them foist one on you if you can avoid it – certainly not without meeting them and getting their views on the project. A good set designer can make you. They potentially wield enormous power. They control the entire visual look of your production. They can also limit your characters' movement with restrictive costumes; they can swamp their performances with over-elaborate sets.

Unless you are a director with a well-developed eye, this early you are probably still very text-bound, not fully visualising the overall look of the thing. Nonetheless, don't let the designer run rampant. At this stage, at all stages, they understandably see things primarily in visual terms. Many of them have strong, stubborn personalities. If they see a brown wall, God help you if you want a pink one. Some have embittered, misunderstood personalities, borne of years of being overlooked by critics who have mistakenly praised the director instead of them.

☞   *Obvious Rule No. 49*
Beware of the Concept.

118

Don't be talked into anything you feel instinctively you'll regret later. If you must have a concept (God save us from that word) then let the concept be something that's worked out between you. Let it spring from the play and not from the fact that the production manager has 500 square metres of black lino left over from their last production. I once heard the fateful words, 'I think it's about time we did something with mirrors.' If at all possible, try and persuade the producer, whoever it is, to let you make as many scenic decisions as late on as possible. There will always be an intense pressure to decide everything before you start. This can be fatal.

In reality, yes, what you do is make the bulk of production decisions long before those key figures, the actors, are even on board. Most of them, though, prefer not to feel like mere passengers on a completed ship, without any say at all as to its course or destination.

I remember a play (not one of mine) where the whole set and furnishings had been completed and sat there awaiting the actors on the very first day of rehearsal. It was like walking into someone else's house. The cast stood awed and anxious. At last one said, rather timidly, 'Are we allowed to move anything?' In my experience, actors are happiest when they feel they have been offered the creative choice of where they sit or how they arrange the room in which they are going to live – or at least feel that they can rearrange it. Often they choose not to exercise that choice, happy to leave it to you, but they like to know the choice is there.

Obvious Rule No. 50
Nobody reads the same script.

Remember that designers often read plays in a totally different way from anyone else; but then each member of the team will approach it slightly differently. Everyone will tend to read the play, naturally enough, from their own specialist viewpoint. An actor will admit this, too. Ask them to read a play first of all with no particular role in mind, and then focusing on a specific part, and their reaction will not surprisingly be very different.

Many designers, especially the busy ones, will skim scripts in search of their own particular areas. Lighting designers will look for such phrases as 'Good morning' and 'Lovely sunny day.' Stage managers will scour the script for 'More tea?' and 'Let me take that heavy case from you.' Wardrobe are interested in 'Get those big muddy boots off, now.'

Designers, it has to be said, even the best of them, sometimes get hold of the wrong end of the stick. Talk to them at length and get in there first. Always get to look at drawings, ground plans and, most helpfully, scale models of what they intend.

Costume designers If the play is heavily costumed you may well need to split the job and find a costume designer. This will be a choice made usually by the designer and the producer. They may well try and rush this thing past you. Make sure you have an input.

As with the set design, get to look at costume drawings well in advance of the actors seeing them, especially with a period play.

☞ *Obvious Rule No. 51*
Beware the manic-depressive costume designer.

What should you look for here? Well, apart from the ability to design costumes that are right for your play (you think I'm joking?), a costume designer should appear friendly, reassuring and sympathetic. Many costume designers, it has to be said, are some of the most eccentric and unbalanced, hysterical members of any team. Some are barking mad. Probably brought on by years of standing wearily in Selfridge's whilst an actor, who's having trouble learning the part anyway, tearfully tries on the whole shop in search of the character neither the author or the director has given them. Be prepared for this. Seek out the sunniest and most even-tempered you can find.

They do exist. You will know you have one of the bad ones if at the halfway point of your rehearsal period, actors are beginning to show unaccountable signs of stress or sudden bursts of hysterics, totally at odds with the otherwise cheerful bonhomie of your rehearsals. Look first to the costume designer. They are probably forcing actors into costumes against their will. And crying if the actor refuses to wear them. This also upsets the people who have actually made the costumes.

It is a two-way thing. Actors, unhappy with the way rehearsals are shaping, will often blame their shoes. This can be an early symptom of greater trouble ahead. 'Not that this scene is ever going to work, I've just seen the costume I'll be wearing.'

Whole wars can be fought on the wardrobe and fitting-room floors, about which you, the director, may have little or no knowledge. It is short-lived ignorance, though, and come the technical rehearsal, it will catch up with you. To my utter mystification, an actor once tore his shirt in half midway through a final rehearsal. It transpired that this was the public result of a long, bitter, private battle between him and the costume designer.

Watch for unaccountable tension. The wardrobe department is a barometer. It is generally, too, the most pressurised and last-minute area. Try and arrange a sneak preview of the clothes – preferably with the actor wearing them, but failing that, a quick glimpse of the costume rail will suffice. Otherwise, by the time you get to see the costumes for yourself with everyone dressed in cerise, it will be far too late.

The lighting designer These days, the list of experts whom a director can call on is lengthening decade by decade as technical know-how becomes more widespread. An established figure is the lighting designer, though even I can remember, way back in my youth, the director (or the producer as he was then known) doing his own lighting with the help of the chief electrician.

Lighting designers (give or take the occasional prima donna) are usually a fairly phlegmatic breed. They are only really directly involved in the production proper around the time that things are at their most frenetic, that is, at the technical rehearsal. In other words, their entire existence is centred round moments of intense activity and near-panic. As directors, most of us face these crises perhaps two or three times a year. A busy lighting designer can experience one a month. The need for a calm temperament is paramount. Seek out ones that sail boats or transcendentally meditate, preferably with a pint in their hand.

Their main weakness, if they have one, is for spending large quantities of your limited budget on equipment. Usually a good production manager or a producer will keep this in check. But beware the lighting designer who approaches you and attempts to enlist your support for a very dramatic lighting effect in Act Two. They are of course attempting to involve you in some hidden battle they are having with those who control the budget.

Similarly, avoid making seemingly innocuous requests to lighting designers. What can seem to you a fairly small-scale idea can be transformed by some designers, especially young and ambitious ones, into huge-scale *son-et-lumière* effects costing thousands. Phrases such as 'starlit night', 'glorious sunset', 'slightly gothic', 'fireworks', 'heat haze', 'long shadows at dusk' can end up blowing your budget to ribbons.

☞ *Obvious Rule No. 52*
Beware the tin briefcase.

Beware what my lighting-designer friend Mick Hughes terms the boys with the tin briefcases. Their eyes throughout are on their PC screens or the lighting positions, but seldom on the play. They are usually at their happiest lighting trade shows or pop concerts rather than pieces of dramatic art, and should be encouraged to do just that. Without exception they will want to fill your stage with smoke. This has nothing to do with anything much except to draw greater attention to their lighting.

A good lighting designer, however, will serve the play, make your actors look good and add atmosphere and texture. Search these out. They are a rare breed.

The sound designer

These are an odd species, often in my experience to be found fast asleep in the stalls during technicals, when not gazing at the screen of their laptop – apparently mixing F/X but actually playing a new video game. They have mobile phones that ring incessantly, as a result of their usually doing two or three jobs at once, one of them in Amsterdam. Many are unaccountably absent when most badly needed. 'He was here a minute ago.' To be fair, they're also a very sociable breed, with a good store of near-libellous anecdotes about disasters they have experienced, and a healthy contempt for most directors, lighting designers and performers. (You will probably, very shortly, be joining that list.)

With the advent of recent sound technology, the thunder sheet, the rain drum and the wind machine are things of the past. The digital sampler and the CD-ROM, the laser and the mini-disc now replace those. At least they did yesterday – things have probably moved ahead by now.

Unfortunately, as with the lighting department, whereas at one time practically anyone with a spare hand could learn to shake a thunder sheet, there are now only a handful of people who can actually understand and operate the new equipment. Most of it is manufactured abroad, with instruction sheets that are either non-existent or written in incomprehensible pidgin English.

☞ *Obvious Rule No. 53*
Never appoint a sound designer unless you intend to use them.

My advice here is to avoid complex recorded sound as much as possible, unless you yourself really understand it or are totally confident in your sound designer. Do not employ one at all unless you really need to. Sound designers will rapidly grow restless at being asked to provide three door knocks and some horses' hooves. Soon your simple production of *Gaslight* will be filled with eerie, wailing muffin men, creaking floorboards and owls hooting incongruously down chimneys.

But in every case, it's all about talking and talking early. Most people are happiest when they've been let into the director's thinking. They're generally happy to go along with this, once they know what it is. Even if they think you're crazy. No one, whatever their department, whatever their experience, can do their best work when they don't know where the whole thing's heading. It's up to you to tell them. And to keep them informed of changes.

Other experts A number of these listed can be very important, depending on the type of show you are doing. If this section seems rather brief, it's because I am dealing primarily here with straight modern plays, and not large-scale classics or musicals.

THE CHOREOGRAPHER
Even a straight play may have a bit of dance in it. If you're not too certain of your own ability to arrange even

a gentle waltz sequence and the actors seem a bit doubt-ful about it, hand it over immediately to a choreographer. Try and select one who's happy to block a two-minute sequence and do three days' work. It can take a load off your mind. On no account leave it to the actors. Unless they're trained ballroom dancers, they will spend ages on it and fret unnecessarily.

THE FIGHT ARRANGER

My advice is to employ one of these if there is any sort of fight required in a play. Actors left to their own devices – even those who boast fight certificates on their CVs – are not necessarily to be trusted to produce an effective, or more important, a 'safe' fight. And safety is the keynote here. Remember that though they may well be able to get it right by themselves once or twice, they will probably have to reproduce it up to a hundred times. Regard fight arranging as choreography with dangerous weapons. Fights need rehearsing and re-rehearsing on a daily basis. Leave time for that. Don't tackle it yourself. You could end up getting sued.

MUSIC

Over the years I have often worked with composers to pro-vide entr'acte and sometimes incidental music for shows. Given the right play, this can be valuable and effective. In my own case, *Henceforward . . .*, *Communicating Doors* and *Comic Potential* all gained enormously from musical input – in the first case from Paul Todd and in the latter two, from John Pattison. Fortunately, thanks to the relax-ing of union demands, it is now possible to include record-ed music in a play. And with the advance of digitised sound this can mean everything from a solo sitar to a whole sym-phony orchestra. Used sensibly and sparingly, it can add a whole new dimension.

If you want to use music under a scene, though, don't leave it till the last minute. Actors do not take kindly to a full symphony orchestra striking up at the technical rehearsal, especially under their carefully rehearsed *sotto voce* love scene. Rather, introduce music early in rehearsal. That way, the actors may actually learn to use it to their advantage and even grow to love it.

Casting So now we have a so-called creative team, made up of our experts from all the various technical departments. (Incidentally, I think the term 'creative team' derives from musical productions – it's a fairly nonsensical one since it fails to include the key creative contributors, the actors. But that's by the by.)

Although the order in which you select these experts may differ slightly, the next step – whether or not you have a star in place – is to cast the play.

☞ *Obvious Rule No. 54*
Casting is everything.

It is my view that this process is the single most important action or series of actions you will make on a production. Most things are reversible, but if you have the wrong actor, however good an actor they may be, in the wrong part, your job as director is reduced to one of damage-limitation specialist.

A few things to watch. Speed. Actors are in general very flexible and used to altering their image. They lose and gain weight, artificially or actually; they can change hair and voice colour like chameleons. They can even appear, some of them, to change their whole physical shape.

What most of them can't do is alter the speed at which they play. Some are mercurial. Others lumber thoughtfully. Try as you might you'll rarely change this. Get it right. Never cast a tortoise as a gazelle or attempt to slow down a cheetah.

Obvious Rule No. 55
Trust your first instincts.

If they read or audition for you, tend to trust your first impressions. Nonetheless, still spend time talking to them if they seem possibly what you're looking for. Look at them in terms not only of the part they might play, but of how they will contrast with other actors you may already have cast. Will they get on? It is not your job to guarantee one big happy family, but a certain respect for each other's work would be a good start.

Don't cast relatives or lovers. Don't cast friends, unless they have become friends as a result of working together previously. Cast some parts with those you know, by all means. It's nice to have a familiar face or two, especially during those early days of rehearsal. But make sure they're right for the part or you may ruin a beautiful friendship. In any event, do try to work with at least fifty per cent new faces every time.

The older a director gets, the more important this becomes. The first sign that directors are in terminal artistic decay is when they start to work with the same people in play after play; the absolute final phase is when a director starts repeating earlier successful productions with the original actors, all of whom are now far too old for the parts.

Obvious Rule No. 56
A refusal should never offend.

Expect to be turned down by actors. Richard Eyre once described the right to say no as the actor's only real power. Once most of them accept the job they're at the mercy of all sorts of elements, many of them beyond their control. So don't hold it against them – certainly not the first half a dozen times they say it to you, anyway. After that, well, assume they might just be trying to tell you something.

Remember, there are always other actors ready to do the job, probably just as well, if differently. Most actors, too, are resigned to being second or even tenth choices. They don't mind. They'd prefer you don't remind them of it, and would certainly rather not be told, as one director once said to an actor, 'I'm scraping the bottom of the barrel, dear.' Nonetheless, it's a fact of life and they know it. They are consoled by the fact that many of the turning points in distinguished careers have come about from second- or fourth-choice casting. And that every time they turn down a part somebody else necessarily becomes second choice to them.

Remember, actors will have a million different reasons for accepting or rejecting a script: from wanting more time with their children, to positively loathing the script.

Stars will be reading it – or initially, I always suspect, skimming it to see how much stage time their character occupies. Having done that, some stars will go through the script again to ascertain how much stage time everyone else's character occupies. If you then get the letter that starts, 'Would that I were young enough to play that wonderful character of the au pair . . .' you'll know that in their opinion the au pair has all the laughs and the best scenes and they want none of it. Whereas, 'I love the play and I wish it well, it's just that I don't feel there's anything I can add . . .' means there's nothing in it for them. 'I'm afraid this is rather old ground as far as I'm concerned' means: You think this play is fresh and original? I did something like it in rep twenty years ago; it didn't work then and it won't work now.

☞ *Obvious Rule No. 57*
Never try to be over-persuasive.

Others, like coy lovers, will ask to meet and be convinced. Personally, I would advise against anyone – director, writer or producer – ever going down this path. Only go with the actor who gives an unhesitating yes to the role. You might possibly be able to argue a reluctant actor round to playing the part eventually. But what you will have created is usually a frail bridge of conviction, which will crack even as the actor steps into the rehearsal room. Self-doubt will emerge the moment they start rehearsing it. They'll have that anyway, but if they are only partially convinced they should be playing the part, then prepare for very rough weather. Remember it is you they will blame: 'Why did I ever let you talk me into doing this?'

Talking of doubt, be prepared for an immediate onset of this yourself the moment the actor has signed the contract. Can they really do the part? Should I have picked actor B instead of actor A? This is normal and perfectly healthy.

Auditions

Some actors you may have worked with before, some (the stars) come pre-packaged, but there will invariably in any show be a few parts for which you will need to meet people and audition. Auditions can be extraordinarily tiring, but are absolutely essential.

Obvious Rule No. 58
Never leave auditions to someone else.

You should even, in West End or Broadway shows, be there to cast the understudies. They are, after all, going to be part of your company, albeit junior members – until your leading lady goes down with laryngitis at the second preview, that is, and they suddenly become the only person standing between you and disaster. It's good then to have someone ready in the wings whom you picked personally and can trust.

Try and allow as much time as possible for meetings. Personally I like at least twenty minutes with each person.

If they're quite obviously wrong this can suddenly become ten to fifteen minutes – which allows twenty-five to thirty minutes for someone really interesting and distinctly possible who comes in next.

Read the play with them at some stage. A lot of actors get to be very good in auditions and can easily fool you, if left entirely to their own devices. They will tap-dance, and sing unaccompanied Irish ballads that will charm you out of the trees, but whether they can play Cordelia for you is a question that will never be answered unless you ask it.

Don't expect a finished performance. Obviously not. But do see if they are even on the right road. Conversely, bear in mind that some of the best actors don't audition at all well.

Whatever happens, try not to hurry people or get impatient (or, as has been known in some cases, downright rude) just because they're not what you're looking for. They've come in specially to see you and you owe them that courtesy. Some actors, admittedly, do behave quite bizarrely, but this is very probably nervousness. Auditioning is never easy, and if they really do want the job it becomes progressively harder. They want to impress you, but at the same time seem neither over-eager nor, on the other hand, to over-compensate by appearing downright uninterested. Sometimes they get it wrong.

An example of this occurred when a young singer once came in to sing for John Pattison and me. She was dressed in a trendy bondage oufit, sort of in keeping with the role for which she was auditioning. But she had scarcely launched into her raunchy up-tempo number when she fainted clean away. The combination of nerves and tight lacing had resulted in severe hyperventilation. Others have been known to burst into tears, get struck dumb, launch into meaningless jokes with no punchline – one actually ruined their chances completely by telling a joke against the director for whom they were reading (bad move!) – or become unaccountably dyslexic.

They sometimes lie – glancing down one actor's CV once, I was surprised to see that he and I had apparently worked together before, though we clearly never had, as he cheerfully acknowledged. (Note: always tailor your CV to fit the person you're seeing.) On another alarming occasion, I recall an actor, elegantly attired in suit and tie, suddenly stripping down to his underpants and string vest (I swear!), dancing to the strains of a cassette player whilst occasionally shouting, 'Fuck you, mother!'

One solemn young girl once launched into a moving soliloquy in which she related her first tender sexual encounter. It clearly was, for she managed to mispronounce the oft-used word 'orgasm' as 'organasm' throughout the entire speech. For my assistant director's benefit, I wrote on my notepad, 'You laugh and you're fired!'

For the director, auditioning is a very tiring, sometimes nerve-racking job. But even if for you it's the twenty-fifth hopeful auditionee you've seen that day, for the actor this is sometimes the first contact they will have had with the remotest possibility of work for weeks, even months. Be patient.

If you're lucky and have the services of a casting director, use them. A good casting director is there to respond to your requirements, to bring actors to your attention whom you've forgotten about or have never even heard of. (Some older casting directors, it's true, can prove a liability, if they've been round the circuit a few times and had major arguments with every actor in Equity.) Casting directors are sometimes feared, sometimes secretly resented by performers who see them as someone who holds their career in their hands. But the best, as I say, are like gold dust.

For various and obvious reasons, never audition alone. Have a second or even third opinion that you trust. When you're meeting or auditioning, if you're male have a woman with you. If you're a woman bring a man along.

They can give you a second view on that most elusive quality of all – sex appeal.

☞ *Obvious Rule No. 59*
People may be equal but they're also different.

We are paddling in the shallows of political correctness here, and although in the eyes of God I'm sure we're all equally desirable creatures, in the eyes of our fellow men or women, alas, we aren't at all. Irrespective of how they are privately, it's a fact of life that some actors exude sex appeal and some don't. That's OK and there's plenty of work for the rest of them so long as you're not looking for Cleopatra or Don Juan. You'll never convince an audience that a character holds the rest of the cast in sexual thrall if they clearly have no such charisma at all.

I need hardly add that sex appeal has nothing whatever to do with looks, shape or size or even age. It's actually that old thing – personality. There are some who only give off this magnetism when on stage. Backstage in the green room they can sometimes seem almost dowdy. Others carry it with them everywhere. Some have it, some don't. It isn't fair but there's no way to legislate for or against it.

If you don't have the luxury of a casting director, you may have to settle for casting with the producer. At all costs – unless they're experienced and to be trusted – try not to involve the author. They're generally very bad judges and, unless they themselves are actors, they'll be looking in that first reading for a finished performance, rather than one that initially shows less but ultimately promises far more. In other words, the average author is expert on the 'what'; you should be allowed the final word on the 'how'.

☞ *Obvious Rule No. 60*
When you're casting, don't try and get clever.

I once sat in with a director who was casting *Romeo and Juliet*. He hit upon the idea of getting all his potential Romeos to read Juliet's role – in order to 'bring out the feminine side of the character'. The problem was, of course, that we ended up with a distinctly feminine Romeo, who made Juliet seem positively butch by comparison. Interesting.

If need be, recall actors you're unsure about. Most of them are happy to be seen again. Sometimes it makes sense to ask an actor you have already cast back to read with a few possibles for the other role. You'll get a better idea that way of the potential chemistry between them.

From personal experience, though, I would advise against asking the actor to join in the final decision-making process. They're not necessarily the best people to consult on this and some of them are actually embarrassed at being requested to cast a colleague whom they'll later be working alongside.

If you are faced with a choice of three possible candidates, try and sleep on it.

Obvious Rule No. 61
There's always someone else somewhere.   ☞

Finally, if you don't see anyone that really fires you, start all over again and prepare to see a load of fresh people. There is almost certainly some unknown out there who is not only available but perfect for the role. Who just happened until last Saturday to be working in Skegness, but is now back in London and raring to go.

I cannot stress enough the importance of auditions.

You are now set. A complete team is on board and you are facing the first day of rehearsal. Be prepared for your initial doubts about the whole project to increase hundredfold as the day approaches.

Before the first rehearsal

What can you do to while away the time?

☞ *Obvious Rule No. 62*
Plan in advance.

Personally, I like to make schedules. Some directors hate this idea and prefer to treat the rehearsal process as a freewheeling event where each day dictates its own agenda. This has its attractions. The very uncertainty of it all tends to bond the company and give them an interest in the project as a whole, rather than in their own particular area.

But be careful. Some directors are so free that they never actually get around to running the show through in its entirety until it is finally before the general public. Understandably this leads to the early preview performances being artistically shaky and technically chaotic.

Fair enough. They are after all, as the director will doubtless point out, only previews, and what do they expect for a reduced-price ticket? The problem is that it is the preview audience which tends these days to be the spark that will either light or fail to ignite the bush fire, which you hope will result in favourable early word-of-mouth publicity. And believe me, no number of brilliant campaigns and poster designs will make up for that. All a poster can do is to tell you a play is on. Word of mouth actually tells you that you will enjoy it.

Anyway, whatever technique of rehearsal planning you use, whether it is detailed advance calls or the casual end-of-day see-you-all-tomorrow-at-ten-then approach, remember that Equity, the actors' union, only allows them to work a certain number of hours a week. And that other departments will also want to call on your actors' time. If you have a star, the press office will descend and demand that in order to promote the show they be taken away for press interviews and photos. The wardrobe department, the wig fitters and whoever else is involved will also want to share the actors with you.

My attitude is to get them all to work to your master plan, rather than you with theirs. If, as director, you fail to secure your own corner, you will find yourself left with no time to rehearse at all. Especially with a musical: the choreographer, the musical director, the wardrobe, wig and shoe departments will have annexed all the time for themselves.

No: plan, plan. Be flexible, be prepared to change it all, and leave yourself leeway within the plan by all means to rehearse areas that aren't developing satisfactorily, but do start with a plan.

You might liken the rehearsal period to a trip downstream. You start at the source, where the currents are gentle, the opportunities for growth infinite. As the days pass, the stream widens and grows deeper. The current quickens and one day, behold, here you are on a full-grown river flowing ever wider, ever swifter. How exhilarating! But do remember this. At the end of it all, just around the final bend, is a huge waterfall, capable of destroying you and your craft in an instant if you are unprepared for it.

That waterfall is otherwise known as the technical rehearsal.

Actors have a curious attitude to directors in general. A sort of mixture of love, loathing and fear. The problem is that generally speaking, they tend to trust directors who have reached a certain age when, as we know, age has nothing particular to recommend it except perhaps a sense of having seen it all before. As Tyrone Guthrie sadly remarked as he reached the end of his career: 'When I was a young man, I was full of exciting and new ideas but it was only with the greatest difficulty that I could persuade an actor to try any of them. Now I am the age I am, having gained some sort of reputation, I could probably get an

The rehearsal period

actor to do almost anything I asked them to. The problem is, I no longer have any ideas.'

But alas, in general it is towards age and experience that most actors turn. It is no guarantee. Most of the time they find themselves in the company of some sort of latter-day Charon, ferryman of the dead, rowing them erratically across the gloomy Styx of a rehearsal period to the land of the dead performance and the dwindling audience.

The first day The best that can be said about this is that it never gets any easier. I have to date directed over 200 plays, both mine and other people's, and I still get nervous. Imagine how the actors feel. By this stage they are convinced that they have been miscast, that their agent has made a dreadful mistake and that the director is going to catch their eye sooner or later and ask, 'Who are you?'

Always be there first to greet everyone, assuring them that, yes, they were exactly whom you were expecting and wanted to see.

In my case I rehearse a play normally for four weeks. I work roughly between ten in the morning and five in the evening each day. I rarely if ever work over the first three weekends. I always run the play on the final Saturday prior to week five, the technical/preview week.

There are various approaches to first days. First there is the usual cup of coffee which serves to mask the absence of the inevitable latecomer: 'Sorry. I'm so sorry. My God! Was there anyone else here on the Circle Line this morning?' Answer: Yes, we all were. We just started out at a sensible time.

After all that there is a multiple choice of how to proceed, ranging from the gentle beginning graduating through to the short sharp shock.

Some directors (I understand) request that no one looks at their script at all for several days, but instead set about bonding the company together with a series of games, improvisations and trust exercises. Volleyballs are sent for and blindfolded actors set about exploring each other through touch. (In my experience most of them get around to that sooner or later, anyway, without any encouragement from me.)

Other directors stand and address the seated company – often, believe it or not, for several days on end. Some sit round a table reading and discussing and exploring for a week or more, physically moving the play around comparatively late on in the rehearsal process.

Some, if the budget allows, take the company off on research trips: to the Imperial War Museum or a block of flats in Brixton. Some arrive with a pile of books to be read at all costs by everyone.

Again, there's no guaranteed right way. All these methods can and have been known to work. In the end, of course, it all depends on the play.

Whatever your approach, remember that time is finite.

Obvious Rule No. 63
Take the plunge.

It is understandable perhaps, given my own role as author/director, that I prefer, particularly when working on my own plays, to employ the sudden shock method. That is to say, we get straight down to the text, sitting round a table on the first morning and reading the thing aloud from start to finish.

The advantage of this is that a lot of people get to hear it read. Not just the actors (though I swear some I have worked with haven't read the entire play properly till then, just their own bit) but all the other relevant elements of the production: stage management, designers, producers, technicians and so on.

Indeed, whenever I start a play in Scarborough at the Stephen Joseph Theatre the circle is even wider than that, with carpenters, publicists, front-of-house staff, box office, finance department, production and administration all attending. It is not unusual in that comparatively small theatre to hold the first reading before an audience of forty or so. A little unnerving for the cast, perhaps, but consider this. Few of those listeners will see the play again until, at the very earliest, a preview. At least between now and then they have some idea of what we're all working on in that rehearsal room.

Actually (and this is peculiar to me, I know), throughout the rehearsal period – unless there are very special circumstances – I have an open rehearsal policy, whereby any member of the theatre is free to come in for a full session and observe the process. To encourage this we had an upstairs gallery built to accommodate such observers.

☞   *Obvious Rule No. 64*
Get it on its feet.

The first read-through completed, in the next session I like to start moving the play around physically, albeit with the actors still with script in hand. I term this a second reading 'on its feet'. Ironically for a writer, I have a great fear of allowing a play to become text-bound. What the characters are saying is important, yes, but what the characters are doing whilst they're saying it is of equal importance. And, of course, what they're *not* saying whilst they're doing it.

There's a category of theatre which has emerged in the last decade or so called 'physical' theatre. I appreciate that it refers to a certain type of approach, but it is in a sense very misleading. It suggests that somewhere there is a non-physical theatre. What theatre isn't or shouldn't be to some extent physical?

I suppose that working predominantly in the round has rather emphasised the importance of this for me. There is, in that type of production, a need for actors to explore physicality early on: both in regard to how they express their own character through their bodies, and also in relation to other actors. The distance, the angle from each other, the area they currently occupy on stage – at the edge, in the middle, hovering nervously at an entrance, sitting, standing, lying down, kneeling – all need early exploration. With an experienced group, a lot of this should be instinctive and can initially be left for them to discover.

Personally, I always arrive with a blank script, with not a single move marked in, and wait for them to make the first move. If they remain static for too long – through inhibition, inexperience or sheer initial terror – then it may become necessary to suggest a move or two. But always, with the proviso that these may – almost certainly will – be changed as the production develops.

It is not unusual by the end of the first week for a production of mine to have been read and given a second reading on its feet – in other words, it has been roughly 'blocked'. It's also probable that we will have gone back to the start and 'walked through' both halves of the play as well. (Walked through as opposed to 'run through', that is, which comes much later – some time after the first 'stagger through'.)

Obvious Rule No. 65
Get an early 'global' view.

By the first weekend, we will have what I term a 'global' view of the play. More importantly, each actor will have some idea, however sketchy, of the journey they will be required to make through the course of the play and of the size of the task ahead of them.

By the start of week two we are ready, therefore, to start again from the top of the play; but this time much more slowly, as we begin to go deeper and explore more thoroughly.

Exploration In many ways this is for me the most tiring time, when I am most in evidence. It's important that everyone understands the play: what they and it are saying and where they as characters fit into the whole scheme of things.

Even in the giddiest comedy, although there is often a great deal of laughter as we work, little mention is made of the comedy itself. The talk is of character, motives and hidden motives, and we explore sometimes quite dark undercurrents. Recently I directed *Mother Figure*, the first of my one-act collection *Confusions*, which can be viewed as a fairly light-hearted extended revue sketch. I caught myself talking about the tendency in some of us to use a relationship, once presumably a loving one, to diminish and debilitate. Or in this instance how a husband can cause his wife to lose all confidence or faith in her own judgement.

Terry And we'll have less of that, too, if you don't mind.

Rosemary What?

Terry All this business about me never going out of the house.

Rosemary It's true.

Terry It's not true and it makes me out to be some bloody idle loafer.

Rosemary All I said I . . .

Terry And even if it is true you have no business saying it in front of other people.

Rosemary Oh, honestly, Terry, you're so touchy. I can't say a thing right these days, can I?

Terry Very little. Now you come to mention it.

Rosemary Niggle, niggle, niggle. You keep on at me the whole time. I'm frightened to open my mouth these days. I don't know what's got into you lately. You're in a filthy mood from the moment you get up till you go to bed . . .

Terry What are you talking about?

Rosemary Grumbling and moaning . . .

Terry Oh, shut up.

Rosemary You're a misery to live with these days, you really are.

Terry I said, shut up.

Rosemary (*more quietly*) I wish to God you'd go off somewhere sometimes, I really do.

Terry Don't tempt me. I bloody feel like it occasionally, I can tell you.

Rosemary (*tearfully*) Oh, lovely . . .

Obvious Rule No. 66
Always be prepared to lose a laugh to keep the truth.

There could be a tendency for the actors, sensing they are in what is essentially a comedy, to seek to lighten that section. There aren't, let's face it, a lot of sure-fire laughs in it. But it is important that they don't, that they keep it serious and true. If not, when the Mother Figure, Lucy, returns to find Rosemary in tears, and starts to console her, first with 'choccy biccies' and then by playing peekaboo with her with a giant doll, the humour will seem forced and shallow. If we believe Rosemary's tears of unhappiness are genuine and that Lucy's long exposure to children has left her treating everyone as children, if the actors can convince us that both those elements are based in truth, then we have the ingredients for the best type of comedy.

LEARNING IT

Unsurprisingly, given my preference for establishing the physical side early on, I generally prefer actors to drop their books as soon as possible. This is not, though, something that I get too insistent upon. The fact is that some actors are blessed with photographic memories, while for others, learning is a difficult and frustrating business. There is also a danger that in learning too fast, they learn inaccurately; and if you've pressured them too much then you've only yourself to blame when they mangle and paraphrase your text. Patient encouragement is the keynote to this, I think.

Early days   To start with, time is on your side. With luck the cast is on your side, too, at this point – why else have they agreed to do the job? Any doubts about you as a director, and the part they've agreed to play in a fit of impetuosity, will have been put into abeyance.

Only stars come with doubts about the text on the first day. This is a ploy to impress on the rest of the company who's really in charge. Where possible, put down such potential confrontations by listening to them with a knowing smile, and have a quiet word in the corner suggesting you talk about it later in private.

DISCOVERING YOUR CAST

☞ *Obvious Rule No. 67*
No two actors work in quite the same way.

Actors, of course, all come with different approaches and it is impossible to generalise about how to deal with them.

Some exude confidence when in reality they have none at all. Others display an engaging diffidence with regard to their own talent in comparison to their fellow performers: 'So-

and-so's brilliant in this, isn't he? I feel like packing my bags and going home right now.' Don't believe it for a second.

There is the worrier, for whom everything is a potential problem. Even coming through the rehearsal-room door and finding a chair to sit on poses an enormous emotional and intellectual challenge. Potentially these can be quite destructive to the overall rehearsal atmosphere, and people will soon start catching their mood if you're not careful. Suggest to the worrier that a good way to approach this particular role is by employing a light-hearted disregard. It sometimes helps. Tell them lies, if necessary, about all the great actors you've ever worked with constantly rolling about with laughter throughout rehearsals. Come to think of it, I think that's actually true.

The worrier is a close relative of the apologiser who stops rehearsals for minutes on end to apologise to all their colleagues, to you, the stage manager, God, the local caretaker who happens to be passing, to everyone, for their appalling inadequacy as an actor. Resist the temptation to say 'Absolutely right', and encourage them to get on with it.

There is the rehearsal hog (not necessarily a star) who by a series of deft manoeuvres manages to place themselves at the centre of all rehearsals, even of scenes they're not in. 'I couldn't help overhearing what you were saying to Harry just now and I wonder how that affects my character . . .?'

For them you need to go into sheepdog mode and isolate them from the rest of the herd. This may mean many weary and often pointless post-rehearsal sessions in the pub alone with them, but at least they're not boring the pants off the rest of the cast.

Obvious Rule No. 68
If an actor's approach works for them, don't try to fix it.
Try to accommodate it.

There are actors who work from the outside in. They need to be able to see themselves – the shoes, their hairstyle, their walk – before they can do the rest of the work. Some directors mistrust these types, claiming they are superficial. Perhaps in some cases this is so, but again, the golden rule is to allow the actor to work in the way they are happiest with if that's the way to get the best results from them.

I certainly tend to prefer this type of actor to the one that works entirely from the inside out. Often you wait tensely for a month for them finally to unveil their creation, only to discover that it is totally wrong.

There was a terrible way of working which was imported from the States a few decades back called The Method. It purported to be based on the teachings of Stanislavsky, insisting that an actor could do nothing until they really and truly felt it, had experienced their character's feelings and emotions.

☞ *Obvious Rule No. 69*
Sometimes you need to fake it.

That approach may be fine for the movies but any stage actor will tell you that in a week of eight performances it just isn't humanly possible to feel it every time. Occasionally, as in life, you need to fake it. A sure-fire test of good acting is how well you can fake it.

The other problem with The Method is that it really requires an actor to work largely in self-absorbed isolation, with no regard for their working colleagues. As the actor mutters, shuffles and mumbles his way through the rehearsal period, giving no indication as to what their final performance will be, no amount of reassurances – 'It's alright, I will get there, don't worry' – are going to help someone who's waiting to play a love scene with them.

Acting is also about sharing, learning to play together.

Good directors never place themselves in the way of this process. Encourage it but keep clear.

Obvious Rule No. 70
Acting is risk taking. Encourage it.

It is important to build trust. Rehearsals are about people – often total strangers – being persuaded to take risks in order to discover how to play the part. This means being given the courage to try something potentially wrong and possibly downright embarrassing, without fear of come-back or ridicule from you, the director, or their colleagues. The lead for this must always come from you.

Rehearsals explore choices. How to cry, how to laugh, how to come into a room, where you stand in that room in relation to other people. During rehearsals you discover how many options there are for one particular moment (usually dozens) and then gradually narrow them down. If an actor trusts you, you will both make the final choice together.

Obvious Rule No. 71
A choice made by the actor is worth five imposed by the director.

If in doubt that it is genuinely going to be a joint choice, always let it be the actor's choice and not yours. If they feel you have reluctantly persuaded them to do something, the result will rarely be as convincing as if they had felt they had chosen it for themselves.

This is not to say that you should make the choice too easily. Actors, especially when they are insecure, will tend to settle for the known, the familiar, the safe – things they have done before and got away with in the past. They joke about this nervously sometimes: 'I'm giving my number forty-one B performance, it never fails. Troubled old man with limp.' Laugh at this, by all means, and then gently lead them away from the tried and trusted cliché.

☞ *Obvious Rule No. 72*
Cast imaginatively when possible.

If they're worth their salt – and if you've got a rehearsal room full of people who genuinely work on forty-one B performances then you've only yourself to blame – they will always respond to anything that might stretch and extend them. Good ones, like athletes, are always looking for a greater challenge, a higher bar to jump. Often, throughout their careers, actors remain lamentably under-stretched. This is sometimes due to insecurity and caution, but more often the result of totally unimaginative casting which requires them, whether they like it or not, to give the same performance over and over again. Television has a lot to answer for in this regard.

Most actors believe they have far more in themselves to give than they have yet given. They look to people like you to unlock that potential. Some will actually work time and again with directors they quite dislike in the belief that, despite this, that particular individual can draw something out of them that other directors can't. Actors are prepared to put themselves through quite a lot to achieve a good performance. It's not a job for the faint-hearted. Believe me, I tried it for eight years.

From all this, it is clear what the bulk of a director's real task consists of: they need the ability to bring together all these disparate talents with their countless different attitudes and working methods, and persuade them to work together harmoniously and with a certain mutual respect. It can be done, but it's sometimes not easy.

As the books go down and the actors begin to gain and maintain eye contact, the interesting part begins, I find. This is the time to start giving more detailed notes.

As you proceed

TIMING

I have mentioned briefly the importance of time allocation and planning and how crucial it is to be ready for the technical rehearsal.

Obvious Rule No. 73
There's a right time to say the right thing.

There is another sort of timing, though, which is just as important. Simply, it's sensing when to give the actor help, information or criticism at just the right time.

Tell them everything in the first day and you'll find yourself repeating it all over again a week later. There is only so much an actor can take in at one time and in the first days there is so much to digest. Bide your time till you sense the actor is receptive. There is always a period when an actor becomes hungry for more information, when they have identified the gaps in their own knowledge of the character. Eventually they'll either turn to ask you or, at the very least, start giving out faint distress signals. Be ready to identify these.

If major rethinking about the character is required, send them home to mull it over at a weekend break, if you can. But don't give them a major thought ten seconds before a final run-through: 'Try playing it for laughs instead' would not go down too well. Timing is crucial: dribble the information to them, a little each day.

Obvious Rule No. 74
Avoid head-on confrontations whenever possible.

If you meet head-on over something – say a small piece of business that the actor is wedded to but you secretly loathe

– allow them right of way. Let them keep it in. Nine times out of ten, the very fact that you've expressed even mild reservations will eventually cause the actor to abandon it of their own accord.

PROXIMITY AND EYE CONTACT

I'm personally rather hot on this, especially working in the round where the two are so important. In the proscenium, actors tend to share eye contact equally between their fellow actors (if they're lucky!), and the audience out front. In the round the majority of the focus is inward; directed to or at least related to each other within the scene.

There is a tendency for actors new to the round to do two things: hold eye contact as much as possible for mutual support, and stand as close together as possible, for the same reason. Help, we're surrounded! It's an understandable thing to do, but it must be discouraged.

Very few of us maintain eye contact for very long. If we do, it should mean something, dramatically: we are in love, we fear attack, we don't understand what they're telling us, we can't believe our eyes. But, in a family, say, where familiarity has bred if not contempt then at least a sort of casual indifference, direct eye contact is far less common. How often is it that when a wife has a new hairstyle, it's her husband who's the last to notice?

☞ *Obvious Rule No. 75*
Let the audience know where the ball is.

This contact or non-contact is important. Mostly it will be instinctive. A well-written scene will tell you when and when not to establish eye contact, but occasionally it needs orchestrating, especially in larger group scenes. The round is about focus: where the cast are looking often dictates where the audience looks.

Obvious Rule No. 76
Keep your distance on stage except when fighting or for-
nicating.

Similarly with proximity. Encourage, where possible, distance between actors, especially on open stages – first, this widens the angle of vision for the audience and second, a small woman standing close to a very tall man doesn't stand a chance of being seen by anyone.

Short actors do have the compensating advantage that, when playing with a taller person, they are obliged to look up, thus being far better lit than the tall actor who is obliged to look down.

Notes

Obvious Rule No. 77
Don't be afraid occasionally to say nothing. (Provided
you don't make a habit of it.)

Never give a note for the sake of it. It takes a lot of bottle to say to an actor, I have nothing to say to you today except well done. But it's infinitely preferable to inventing something. If necessary ask them if they've anything to say to you. They might have a question of their own which they're nervous about or feel a little foolish for asking.

A lot of directing is common sense. Try never to finish a day on a negative low. If the actors have just done the world's worst run-through, it doesn't really help to spell it out to them in painful detail for a hour afterwards. They know. Telling them you have never worked with such an untalented bunch is liable to lead to sleepless nights and an even worse run-through tomorrow. Laugh and offer to buy them a drink.

Far better to leave recriminations for a new day when things have cooled down a little. Good morning, untalented bunch.

Much, too, as I have said, is to do with sensing and sensitivity. When to say what – and how to say it. Better, of course, to tell an actor how much you like the positive things they're doing and encourage those, rather than to stamp all over the bad bits. A bright actor will soon deduce that the bit you have pointedly not been praising might not altogether be meeting with your approval. A good actor would probably have discarded it anyway, but they must be given the freedom to try things for themselves.

Occasionally, a difficult moment requires what I term temporary assistance – a prop, a piece of business to give the actor the initial momentum to achieve something. If they feel unconvincing playing a speech on the floor, encourage them to stand on the table. Ultimately, you might jointly decide that the floor is better after all, but chances are that the blockage will have been cleared.

Sometimes, alarmingly, a performer will start developing a performance with which they are genuinely delighted but which is so totally out of tune with the play, the other performances or the overall style of the production, that you will feel the urge to rush from the room in despair.

Resist this temptation at all costs.

☞ *Obvious Rule No. 78*
Acknowledge that there are some relationships that are
non-beneficial for both of you. You can't win them all.

Nothing is irreversible, though; sometimes you may find yourself drastically altering and rebuilding a performance. It's always a tricky task telling an actor that virtually every choice they have made so far is utterly wrong. Moreover, telling them this bluntly in one session could result in a terrible loss of confidence. Be selective with your criticisms. Spread them out. Liken it to rebuilding a card house, one card at a time. It will take days, iron nerve and a steady hand. Of course, if you'd been more alert, you'd have spotted all this a lot earlier.

Make a note not to continue this relationship in the future. There is nothing more depressing for either of you than to be dealing entirely in negatives. In general seek out the actors to whom you can generally say: yes, Yes, YES! Fortunately for actors there are dozens of different directors, who tend to say yes to different things.

Select when to give public notes – restrict these to general points or work that needs doing on group scenes – as opposed to one-to-one private notes for a single individual's ears only. Actors often appreciate the chance to discuss their role away from the other performers. Some genuinely don't want to take up valuable rehearsal time talking about themselves; which is laudable; all the same, sometimes they need the talk.

They may have a concern about how a scene is progressing or have secret reservations about what they're getting from the actor they're playing opposite: not exactly criticisms, just things like, 'If he plays it that fast I don't get time to make the emotional switch that the scene requires me to do.' With a regular company these issues will get discussed directly between the actors themselves (always the preferable option) without fear of them offending each other. But a new company may turn to you, the director, to regulate.

Obvious Rule No. 79
It helps to be a bit of an actor yourself.

Often there's a need for diplomacy and bridge-building if potential differences develop between individual actors. Whatever you do, don't let them try to draw you into an alliance with one against another. Remember you are Solomon. It's fair enough to arbitrate, but don't join in the stone throwing.

☞ *Obvious Rule No. 80*
Try never to make people look or feel stupid. You'll lose
their trust.

Sometimes though, privately, all an actor really wants is to
discuss something they feel silly bringing up in front of the
others. One used to draw me aside regularly to ask, in an
urgent whisper, how the next word was correctly pro-
nounced. In the best-run rehearsals, though, no one should
feel silly about bringing up anything.

☞ *Obvious Rule No. 81*
A lot of acting is purely instinctive. Respect that.

A lot of actors these days are highly educated, but there are
still some who left school early and ever since have carried
a slight inferiority complex about their interrupted educa-
tion. There is no necessity for an actor to be educated at all
(though it helps to be able to read). Some of the least
'brainy' ones I know can play a nuclear physicist or a university professor with convincing ease.

I haven't a great deal of time for directors who refuse to
allow something quite magical to exist without demanding
that the actor dismantle it to prove that they know how
they did it. They remind me of those terrible maths masters
at school who demanded to see all your working-out.
Sometimes, I would protest, I just guessed right.

One small rule: never, never give an inflection except as
a last resort. The thing will always stick in their throat for
ever. 'I didn't *know* that you were a postman.' 'I didn't
know that *you* were a postman.' It may take half an hour
to get them to say it via another route, but it'll be worth it.

Personally, I prefer to lead as a director by parable and
example. My feeling is that an appropriate anecdote or a
sharp graphic image will generally lead an actor closer to a
feeling, an experience, than any amount of direct instruc-

tion. Better to tell an actor to enter the room as if announcing a sudden death, than to go into detail about tiptoeing and using hushed tones. That way, the actor will take the image and interpret it in their own way. A childhood story, likewise, will often spark off an equivalent story for the actor and subsequently help them to generate the right mood. I like to regard these as 'trigger' images.

Obvious Rule No. 82
Try not to demonstrate too much.

It's a great temptation.

Whenever possible, always allow the actor to dictate the running. As they work with you more and grow to trust you, they will be prepared to show you more and more of their first instincts. Generally, with good actors, these are ninety per cent right. The rest you can work on, or negotiate over.

Comedy

If you are directing a comedy the first day or so will be filled with laughter, as actors hopefully enjoy first the read-through (where the laughter is often quite nervous) through the early days as they uncover the character layers and the situation details.

Allow the laughter. It relaxes everyone and swiftly creates a good working atmosphere. Inevitably, as the play is revisited and repeated, the jokes wear thin and the laughter dries up. It's at this point that some actors get the secret fear that they've somehow 'lost it'. Of course, what's really happened is that everyone's no longer finding it funny.

There'll be an enormous temptation to up the level of the playing in order to regain the lost laugh. Discourage this at all costs.

☞ *Obvious Rule No. 83*
When directing comedy, don't whatever you do lose your
nerve.

I have seen cases where not just individual actors but an entire production appears to have panicked and abandoned all sense of truth. This is inevitably a sign that the director has experienced a loss of nerve and has encouraged the actors into excesses.

☞ *Obvious Rule No. 84*
Trust the script.

Presumably you liked it enough at the read-through, or why are you doing it? When directing my own work, as I've indicated, I make it a rule never to talk about the laughs and where they might or might not come. There's nothing more dispiriting for an actor than to be told to hold that next line for a second, as there's bound to be a tremendous laugh there – only to find that the moment passes in dead silence during the first performance.

No, I much prefer a few lines to be lost sometimes at a preview because the actors were taken by surprise at the reaction. They'll be ready for it second time around.

☞ *Obvious Rule No. 85*
Concentrate on the truth of the scene. Let the comedy
take care of itself.

Besides, the plain fact is that in theatre, no two audiences are ever quite the same. Sometimes they vary so much that it's difficult to believe that we're all doing the same play. Certainly with my own stuff which often hovers uneasily between light and dark it would be fatal to start allowing for so-called laughter points: at some performances laughter seldom occurs.

As a broad principle, then, when directing a comedy search for the seriousness. When directing a drama, on the other hand, seek out every scrap of legitimate humour.

Later days

Obvious Rule No. 86
Run-throughs are helpful.

As the rehearsal period draws to a close, plan to run sections of the play as often as possible: whole scenes, then whole acts and finally the whole play. A performer, particularly one with a large part, will appreciate this. Like runners, they need to know how to pace themselves, to sense where the rest points are and where the variations of pace need to occur; to judge what emotional reserves they'll need to play the last few pages, say.

In a play with several scenes and frequent time changes, an actor also needs to know – following a quick costume change, perhaps – at what level to pitch the next scene. Like a singer, they have to find the right note, if you like. They may have left the stage at the end of scene one in deep despair, but they are now returning at the top of scene two, elated at good news they've just received. It helps if they can fix this emotional map in their head – so that when a zipper jams in the wings they don't completely lose sight of their performance.

In the last stages, one or two strangers will enter the rehearsal room to watch a run. These will include technicians, stage managers, production staff and designers. Most of them will sit through your minor masterpiece in glum silence, staring at their clip boards. Do not be discouraged. They will be concentrating on areas that concern them, rarely on the play as a whole. They will be asking themselves questions, like 'Is he really going to bang the plate down that hard?', 'If she's going to stand there I'll have to re-rig half the grid to light her', 'I'll have to buy her some different underwear if she's going to fling herself about like that.'

Be of good cheer and reassure the actors accordingly. Later you will, if you're lucky, see these same Jeremiahs transformed at the first preview into beaming visions: their lighting problems resolved, their precious props safe and sensible underwear in place.

IN CONCLUSION

During your rehearsal period, expect bad days when nothing seems to progress at all. Expect days when you appear to have taken a giant step backwards. We got it right yesterday, what happened? Remember, such days might just mark the prelude to you all heading in a new, exciting direction tomorrow. To compensate, there will be the days when it all goes suddenly, wonderfully, inexplicably right. Get enough of these days under your belt and you'll be well and truly ready for your technical rehearsals.

If you've planned it right, the company will by then be raring to go. Whatever doubts they have – hopefully small ones – will be overshadowed entirely by the desire finally to get in front of an audience. If this is the case, you may be allowed a small moment of self-congratulation at having brought things to a climax at just the right moment.

Now, you are about to leave the rehearsal room for the last time, and early next week you will be on stage, hopefully with the set in place.

FRATERNISING: A FOOTNOTE

☞ *Obvious Rule No. 87*
If you can't hold your liquor, never drink with actors.

A small warning. There is always a temptation if the rehearsals are going well to want to become 'one of the lads'. Actors, especially younger actors in a strange town, will want to live it up a bit: to try the local pubs and clubs, to carouse till dawn. What the hell, it's what being an actor is all about, don't begrudge them that. But don't be tempted, either, to join them on these all-night binges. Directors tend rapidly to lose their credibility once they've got hopelessly drunk and been carried home to bed, having made a pass at half the cast or been sick on their shoes. Actors know at heart that directors are human beings and as fallible as the next person. But they also need to retain a grain of hope that the one leading them has a modicum of divine vision. It's lonely sometimes at the top.

The DSM

Obvious Rule No. 88
A good DSM is like gold.

I have left one of the most important elements of a successful rehearsal period till last. The DSM (Deputy Stage Manager), especially in smaller-scale repertory theatres like the Stephen Joseph Theatre, will be the only other person continuously in the room with you from the start to finish of the rehearsal-room period. He or – more often it seems these days – she will notate, report, prompt and generally run the rehearsals on a technical level, ensuring that things proceed smoothly. Other colleagues, namely the Stage Manager and ASM (assistant stage manager), will be less in evidence, involved as they are in the assembling of props, small items of furniture and occasionally even in the construction of various items.

The working relationship you have with your DSM is important. Few will wish to intrude on the artistic side, unless asked, but they can help to point out the occasional inconsistency which you and the actors have overlooked: 'He handed his umbrella to the porter in scene three. How can he still have it?' Their role ranges from this sort of thing, right through to a smile of encouragement when a scene suddenly takes off for the first time. We all need a bit of that.

The DSM is also very useful when it comes to gently reminding an actor for the fifth time that they have their main speech in Act One entirely back to front. It's an unpopular job, but someone has to do it.

☞ *Obvious Rule No. 89*
Be prepared.

The DSM is often the production's lifeline to the outside world and keeps the rest of the team informed as to production changes and updates. A rehearsal report is issued each day: 'The dining table will need to be strong enough to stand on,' 'Miss Wilkins needs wellington boots for the start of scene three.'

Work on maintaining a good relationship between you and the DSM; share every detail. Once you get into the theatre, and especially during that fraught period known as the technical rehearsal ('the tech'), the well-briefed DSM, fully appraised of your intentions, can save your life.

Technicals

☞ *Obvious Rule No. 90*
The technical rehearsal is no time for surprises.

Try and sort out as many of the technical matters as you possibly can before the technical rehearsal. Bludgeon your designer or production manager into giving you as many bits of set as they can muster.

If they tell you that there's no way you can have things, then demand detailed mock-ups which you can use in the rehearsal room. Often this does the trick nicely, as faced with the option of building something twice – after all, what's the difference between a rehearsal staircase and a performance staircase? Answer, not a lot – they will settle for building it just once in half the time in order to shut you up.

Especially in a period play, persuade your cast to don approximately the right clothes (rehearsal skirts and so on) throughout the rehearsal period. The good actors always will, but the one who doesn't bother is always the one that most needs to: she's the one who puts on the period corset at the dress rehearsal and promptly hyperventilates during her long speech, fainting clean away and holding things up for hours.

PROPS

Stage managers as a breed are deeply mistrustful of actors, especially actors in rehearsal. Moreover, their suspicions are not always groundless: actors can be notoriously careless with carefully constructed items that have taken the prop room days to create. As a result, stage managers are pleased enough to work on your props but reluctant to hand them over to the actor until the very last minute, preferably at the technical rehearsal. Try and break down this mistrust if you can. If an actor is going to break a prop, it may well be during a nervous technical rehearsal because it is unfamiliar. If the stage management department flatly refuses to hand over their treasures, however, then demand that the cast are given accurate rehearsal props.

SOUND

Obvious Rule No. 91
Introduce the sound as early as you can.

Make friends with the sound people. Lighting must necessarily wait till the technical, but sound you can hear in advance and can even, if you have the equipment available, play in a modified form in the rehearsal room at final run-throughs. This also allows you an opportunity to cut the sound department's excesses, privately and tactfully rather than before the full public scrutiny of their sniggering colleagues at the technical. Humiliate nobody if you can avoid it. Their revenge will be terrible if you do.

LIGHTING

☞ *Obvious Rule No. 92*
Try and give a clear brief to the lighting designer.

Make sure your lighting designer not only sees the run but that you talk through the whole play with them. Don't tell them how to do their job (they won't love you for that) but you should tell them the overall impression that you're hoping to see. Give them as clear and concise a brief as you can manage. No brief at all from a director is the most frustrating and time-consuming thing a lighting designer can contend with. It can also prove expensive, since they'll probably order in enough equipment to cover all contingencies.

☞ *Obvious Rule No. 93*
Do anything to make the transition from rehearsal room to the stage as gentle as possible.

If you can get your actors near the stage for a quick run-through of the play prior to the tech, however faltering, this will also help. Usually this is impossible as there's another show in the auditorium, with a vast and immovable permanent set. But rehearsing, especially in the later stages, in the space you are eventually going to be playing in can be invaluable. If this is impossible then do go into the auditorium and sit there yourself – in different seats, everywhere in the house. Try and see a show in there. Check the sightlines. Check the acoustics. Ask the actors who are currently playing there for their impressions. Seek out the director if you can. Persuade your own actors to do the same.

However prepared you are, be ready for everything you have achieved over the weeks of rehearsal to disappear entirely the minute you start the technical period. Actors will develop extraordinary temporary mannerisms. They will laugh at each other, at their props and costumes. They will stare at the stage lanterns and move exaggeratedly round the stage as if in search of light. They will start in amazement at your delicately placed sound effects and ask questions about the set like 'Is this how it's going to be, then?' Despite your careful rehearsal room mark-out they will nonetheless display stunned amazement at the fact that the window is over there and the room has a step in the middle of it. Ignore all this. It's a technical rehearsal and the play, momentarily, must go on the back-burner. All the actors need do is stand where they're going to be standing, doing roughly what they're going to be doing, saying lines they're roughly going to be saying.

Obvious Rule No. 94
Never be tempted to start re-rehearsing scenes during a technical.

There are dozens of very expensive technical people and stage crew out there. To stop suddenly for an ad hoc rehearsal results in everyone else having to stop. Now is not the time.

The auditorium will fill up with people you have never seen before. In a large theatre, many of these are dressers or wardrobe assistants or scenic assistants. They will gaze at the play in blank disbelief as if to say, 'We have been working all hours for *this*?' This potentially causes an inexperienced director no end of self-doubt. My advice is to ignore them. Their frowns are about uneven hemlines or unpainted areas of backcloth and are nothing to do with the play, to which they often remain passionately faithful, months after you the director have gone off the whole production and are away working in Bournemouth.

The ideal tech is the one where the actors come and go and are in the bar two hours earlier than they expected to, leaving you and the technical team in peace to the business of getting the technical bits right.

Remember that in all this, the one key person at this stage is still your faithful DSM.

☞ *Obvious Rule No. 95*
Pray your DSM is up to the job.

Now, from their perch in the prompt corner or control box, their role changes. They will direct all systems via cue lights or spoken commands. If they are doing their job well, all your troubles are halved. If you hit the rare (in my experience very rare) bad DSM, cut your losses now and remove all the cues (lighting, music, sound or practical ones) that you possibly can – that is if you don't want a dog barking every time the phone's supposed to ring.

Above all, *keep calm*. There will be a million reasons to get wound up. Huge pauses will occur when the stage remains empty and nothing seems to be happening. Trust your stage manager that something constructive is happening. Put your feet up in the stalls and indulge in a little reminiscence with the design team. They will have tales to tell about technicals that make your small delays pale into insignificance.

If the delay continues wander down and chat to the cast. They like to know you still care.

☞ *Obvious Rule No. 96*
Don't stop unless you have to.

When the technical is under way, if nothing appears to be going wrong, let it run. There may be snags going on backstage, but if nobody calls a halt these might all be taken in hand. There's certainly nothing less constructive than a director calling a halt simply because everything *is* going smoothly.

A technical is like a large liner. Once it does stop, it takes an age to get up a head of steam again, as all departments from the flies to the sound department are stood by and made ready to go again.

Should you hit a sticky problem that looks as if it will take at least forty minutes to solve, be prepared to bypass it and solve it at a separate session later. The longer a technical is allowed to go on, the more tired people get and the slower it becomes. Besides, your actors are precious. Get them off the stage as soon as you can and home in bed. They'll have their time at the dress rehearsal tomorrow.

Hopefully you'll get at least two of these. The first one is really a consolidatory technical rehearsal. If you had to stop and start a number of times at the technical, it will be the first opportunity the stage management, crew and technical staff will have had to run the play in uninterrupted real time. It's the first occasion when they'll get a proper sense of how swiftly cues are coming at them and how long they have for scene or quick costume changes.

Dress rehearsals

Nonetheless it is perfectly fair for you now to turn your attention back to the actors, keeping just a quarter of an eye out for technical discrepancies you might have missed during the technical.

For the actors, the most pressing concern is to adjust their individual performances so that they begin to reach out and fill the house. After the misleading cosiness of the rehearsal room, the empty theatre, however intimate, will nonetheless appear huge. Often the company will lament that they have 'lost it all', that they feel they're just shouting, that all the careful nuances they had developed between them seem to have been dissipated.

You may need to do a great deal of hand-holding at this stage. Last week they were an eager company who couldn't wait to get on stage. Now they're sullen children who want to go back to their reassuring rehearsal room.

I tend to say to them at this time – but only if I genuinely mean it – that what they're doing is so good, in my opinion, that it seems a shame if they don't try to share it with the audience.

See if you can't get a few people in for the second or, if you're lucky, third dress rehearsal. Even a handful of strangers is better than nothing.

Previews Your technical rehearsal is over. Your dress rehearsals have passed and hopefully the show is in reasonable shape. After two dress rehearsals or so the play will gradually begin to reassert some of the qualities it had during its last days in the rehearsal room.

☞ *Obvious Rule No. 97*
The first preview changes everything.

If you are lucky your next time through the play will be the first preview.

If you are unlucky, your first performance will also be your so-called press night. If you are really unlucky and your technical has overrun by several sessions, your first full continuous run of the play will be the press night itself – this has been known. In this case, the chances of everything running smoothly are remote. Brace yourself for actors to stumble on half-dressed after an abortive quick costume change and for sudden unplanned blackouts to occur during your grand dénouement due to unexplained glitches in the computerised lighting board.

But whatever happens, with the first preview over, from now on you will begin to feel those first pangs experienced by every director: a feeling of faint redundancy, like that of a ship's pilot who has managed to guide a ship out of port, through the treacherous river channel to the open sea which now lies ahead. Your job is nearing completion and it is time for the crew to put you ashore.

How they choose to do this will depend very much on how they rate your navigational skills and man management. Some directors are piped affectionately ashore; others are thrown unceremoniously overboard.

Once the previews have started, the relationship between you and your acting crew will undergo a considerable change. Until now, if you have established any sort of trust between you at all, your views will usually be accepted. After all, yours is the only outside view the actors have had. Once performances start, there will be hundreds of views. Moments you had all privately anticipated would be hilarious, sections in which you promised they'd be able to hear a pin drop, don't achieve any such effect at all. Silence greets the great comic moment and giggles are clearly heard during your dramatic climax. Girlfriends, wives, mistresses and, worse still, fellow actors (some with a personal axe to grind) turn up and tell your cast that they're too slow, too quiet, too fast, badly dressed or underlit.

If individual moments aren't working on a regular basis (for audiences do vary enormously and another night it might suddenly work) you would do well to admit your share of the blame immediately. Indeed, try to point it out before the actors point it out to you – which they undoubtedly will do. In other words, be prepared to shoulder the blame with them. In that way you might lose a few battles but with luck you could still be there to help them win the war. If there are bullets flying, they appreciate a general who's prepared to take his place in the firing line beside them.

If the play is going reasonably well, a lot of what isn't working will be corrected by the actors themselves over the next few days. They will get the feel of the stage, start to play the auditorium, pitch their performances to suit their surroundings. They'll make dozens of tiny adjustments to compensate for the live nature of the event. That's their job.

☞ *Obvious Rule No. 98*
Keep the company together.

Arrange to meet regularly during the afternoons of previews even if there doesn't appear to be much to say and even if it's only for an hour. Often, the actors will have concerns which have only arisen as a result of live performance: Why isn't that happening? Do you think they're understanding this? There will always be something to discuss and if necessary correct. Besides, if they enjoyed the rehearsals they may actually want to see you. As far as the play's concerned, the jury is still out and they need each other's company. They need to have time together other than on stage. It's up to you to arrange that.

☞ *Obvious Rule No. 99*
Encourage the actors to keep their innocence.

It's about this time too, especially with comedy, that I find myself exhorting the company to keep their innocence. I liken the audience to kerb-crawlers cruising the streets and imploring innocent, truthful actors to climb on board in return for honeyed promises of rich rewards. I tell them they should resist this at all costs – they should never pander, never at any price yield to temptation. For what the audience are asking or appear to be encouraging is that they broaden their performance, abandon its truth, all in return for a little more laughter.

But the wicked audience are not to be trusted. If you yield to them they will take you for the shortest possible ride and then dump you unceremoniously back in the street. Their belief in you will have gone and their laughter will stop.

It's difficult to hold on sometimes, and ironically it is almost harder for the experienced actor than it is for the newcomer who very often daren't stray far from the allotted path. By contrast an experienced actor, given a speech of ten lines, can weave miracles with it as the weeks progress. Through timing, stress and delivery they can transform what was a straight piece of dialogue with a good laugh at the end of it into a speech dotted with ten smaller laughs. Clever – but ultimately self-defeating, for the speech is now so fragmented that no one has a clue what it means as a whole.

Years ago, I worked with a very solemn young actress who played a small but significant role in a new play of mine. She sat through rehearsals watching everything gravely and intently. She rarely needed much help from me, because her instinct for the character and natural timing were brilliant.

On the first night she had the audience in fits of laughter every time she opened her mouth. So much so that I broke one of my unwritten rules and went backstage in the interval to congratulate her.

To my alarm I found her in front of her dressing-room mirror in floods of tears. Very concerned, I asked her what was wrong.

'I'm sorry,' she said, 'I can't stop them laughing.'

I gently explained to her that it was my intention that they should laugh. She looked at me amazed. 'It was?'

A couple of days later I came back to see the show again. All the laughter had gone, along with her innocence and credibility. She was mugging shamelessly. Alas, she had 'discovered' comedy. It took us some weeks to recapture her performance.

SEEING THEM OFF

As a writer-director, I find this time especially poignant. I have, after all, lived with the characters from birth, as it were: through the initial casting of their actor and future interpreter, the introduction of the actor and character to each other and the subsequent growth of the relationship in rehearsal, to this, the final handover. A moment of separation: most of the character is now the actor, but inside them goes a very tiny part of me.

Press night
☞ *Obvious Rule No. 100*
With critics you sometimes get more than you deserve, you sometimes get less than you deserve. You never ever get what you deserve.

Theatre puts itself through an ordeal known as the press night, when as many critics as possible are invited, both local and national. We then wait in nervous apprehension, overnight or even longer, to learn what they all thought of it.

There are critics who love the theatre, who manage to express a sort of positive enthusiasm for the theatrical craft even with shows they dislike, and despite having had a wretched evening, remain infectious, enthusiastic and lacking in malice.

On the other hand, there are those who neither know nor care about theatre. They are disgruntled sports writers or fashion reporters, doubtful poets or failed dramatists, who've been promoted sideways into what their editor considers to be a fairly harmless area – rather as prime ministers tend to reward colleagues who have fallen from grace by making them arts ministers.

Many of us in the theatre spend our lives being concerned about the views of such people. My advice is don't. Be grateful for the good or constructive ones and disregard the bad ones. If possible read neither, certainly not until much later. Life's too short.

Remember a press night is not going to be a typical performance. It is filled with people with vested interests. Agents, mothers, spouses. Critics taking up two seats (though they usually only sit in one).

The rest are the producer's friends and relations, who laugh far too loudly, having been filled full of free drink beforehand. On press nights in London, the curtain traditionally goes up at 7 p.m., but although the majority of the audience attends such events regularly, twenty per cent of them usually arrive late, resulting in the start being delayed for ten minutes or more. The interval goes on for half an hour because they're all talking so loudly that no one hears the intermission bells – by which time few can remember what the first act was about in any case.

At the end, if it's a very glitzy first night, full of celebrities, you may receive a standing ovation – the first and last you will ever get. However, you won't get this from the critics, who will be racing from the building as if in response to some personal fire alarm the moment the play has ended.

After all these delays, not surprisingly, the curtain comes down at more or less its usual time, despite the early start.

Afterwards

Party by all means. You'll know in your heart if the show went well. If it did, celebrate. The critics may still hate it, but if you're happy then enjoy the moment. These occur all too rarely and are to be treasured.

Obvious Rule No. 101
No one ever set out to do a show with the intention of giving you a bad time.

If you feel it hasn't worked, it is even more important to gather up your troops and restore morale. Unless you're playing Broadway where shows literally do vanish overnight, the cast have to return again and again, playing to a dwindling number of punters, night after night, till the merciful end of the scheduled run. It can be very dispiriting – like attending a funeral and then having to wait till the corpse has properly died. Yet I'm constantly amazed at how actors can make a positive experience even out of this. It's all they can do, I suppose.

The consolation is that the greater the disaster, the better the anecdotes will be later. After all, whoever heard an actor start a good story with the words, 'I was in this very successful show . . .'? No, theatre folklore is based largely around disasters. They are the shows that unite us as companies, the ones that contain our funniest, fondest memories. Like the London cockneys who bemoaned the loss of the camaraderie after the end of World War Two, we all need a disaster or two in our lives to bring us closer together.

AND FINALLY . . .

When the dust dies down, if you've done your job properly and the production is successful, don't be disappointed if you the director are dismissed in a single line in most reviews: 'Keeps a firm hand on proceedings', 'Maintains a giddy pace', etc.

Rejoice in the reviews of others, especially your actors. For the important thing is that you and they know how important your contribution has been.

Chronology of plays

1976	Just Between Ourselves	SLT, January
		Queen's Theatre, London, April 1977
1977	Ten Times Table	Stephen Joseph Theatre in the Round (SJTIR), Scarborough, January
		Globe Theatre, London, April 1978
1978	Joking Apart	SJTIR, Scarborough, January
		Globe Theatre, London, March 1979
1979	Sisterly Feelings	SJTIR, Scarborough, January
		Olivier Theatre, NT, London, June 1980
	Taking Steps	SJTIR, Scarborough, September
		Lyric Theatre, London, September 1980
1980	Suburban Strains (*musical*)	SJTIR, Scarborough, January
		Round House, London, February 1981
	Season's Greetings	SJTIR, Scarborough, September
		Apollo Theatre, London, March 1982
1981	Way Upstream	SJTIR, Scarborough, October
		Lyttelton Theatre, NT, London, October, 1982
	Making Tracks (*musical*)	SJTIR, Scarborough, December
		Greenwich Theatre, London, March 1983
1982	Intimate Exchanges	SJTIR, Scarborough, June
		Greenwich Theatre, London, June 1984
		Ambassadors Theatre, London, August 1984
1983	It Could Be Any One of Us	SJTIR, Scarborough, October
1984	A Chorus of Disapproval	SJTIR, Scarborough, May
		Olivier Theatre, NT, London, August 1985
1985	Woman in Mind	SJTIR, Scarborough, May
		Vaudeville Theatre, London, September 1986
1987	A Small Family Business	Olivier Theatre, NT, London, May
	Henceforward . . .	SJTIR, Scarborough, July
		Vaudeville Theatre, London, November 1988
1988	Man of the Moment	SJTIR, Scarborough, August
		Globe Theatre, London, February 1990
	Mr A's Amazing Maze Plays	SJTIR, Scarborough, November
		Cottesloe Theatre, NT, London, March 1993
1989	The Revengers' Comedies	SJTIR, Scarborough, June
		Strand Theatre, London, October 1991
	Invisible Friends	SJTIR, Scarborough, November
		Cottesloe Theatre, NT, London, March 1991
1990	Body Language	SJTIR, Scarborough, May
	This is Where We Came In	SJTIR, Scarborough, August
	Callisto 5	SJTIR, Scarborough, December
1991	Wildest Dreams	SJTIR, Scarborough, May
		The Pit, London, December 1993
	My Very Own Story	SJTIR, Scarborough, August
1992	Time of My Life	SJTIR, Scarborough, April
		Vaudeville Theatre, London, August 1993

1992	Dreams From a Summer House	SJTIR, Scarborough, August
1994	Communicating Doors	SJTIR, Scarborough, February
		Gielgud Theatre, London, August 1995
	Haunting Julia	SJTIR, Scarborough, April
	The Musical Jigsaw Play	SJTIR, Scarborough, December
1995	A Word from Our Sponsor	SJTIR, Scarborough, April
1996	The Champion of Paribanou	SJT, Scarborough, December
1997	Things We Do For Love	SJT, Scarborough, April
		Gielgud Theatre, London, March 1998
1998	Comic Potential	SJT, Scarborough, June
	The Boy Who Fell Into A Book	SJT, Scarborough, December
1999	House & Garden	SJT, Scarborough, June
	(two separate but connected plays)	Royal National Theatre, London, August 2000
2000	Virtual Reality	SJT, Scarborough, February
	Whenever	SJT, Scarborough, December
2001	*Damsels In Distress:*	
	GamePlan	SJT, Scarborough, May
	FlatSpin	SJT, Scarborough, July
	RolePlay	SJT, Scarborough, September
2002	Snake In The Grass	SJT, Scarborough, June